Martin Storey's
scandinavian
knits

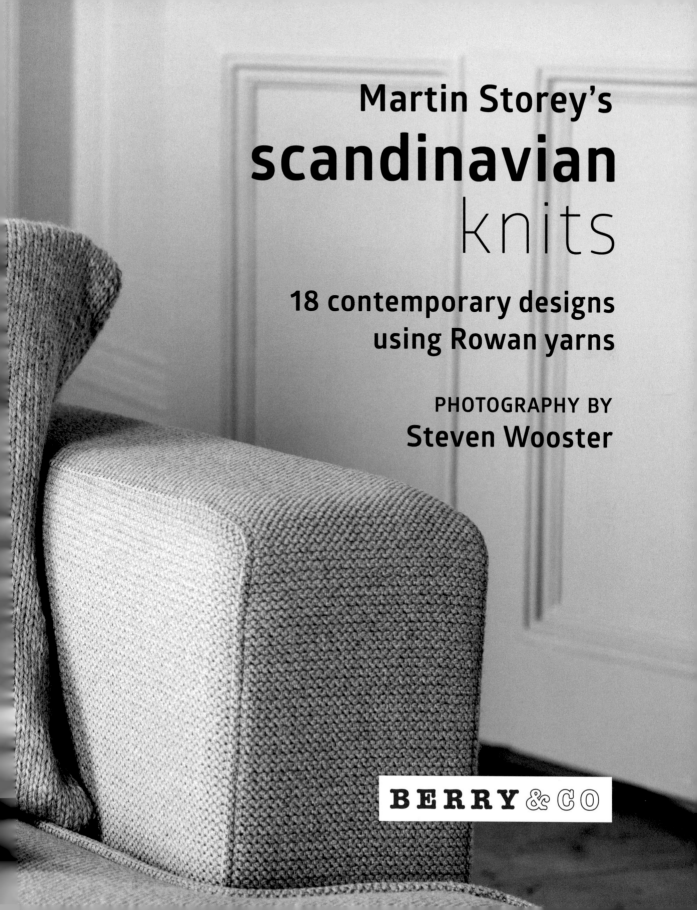

Martin Storey's
scandinavian
knits

18 contemporary designs using Rowan yarns

PHOTOGRAPHY BY
Steven Wooster

BERRY & CO

Martin Storey's Scandinavian Knits
First published in 2016 by Berry & Co (Publishing) Ltd
47 Crewys Road
London NW2 2AU

Design: Anne Wilson
Pattern writing (and knitting): Penny Hill and Martin Storey
Pattern checking: Jill Gray
Charts: Anne Wilson
Styling: Susan Berry
Special photography (pages 10, 13, 14 left, 16, 22, 25 right,
27 right, 32, 36 right, 41, 43 right, 96): Hazel Young

British Library Cataloguing in Publication Data
A catalogue record of this book is available
from the British Library.

ISBN 978-0-9927968-3-9

Printed in China

contents

Introduction   6

THE PROJECTS

Rune bed runner   8, 44

Christa hat   10, 48

Frode cushion   12, 50

Thora scarf   14, 52

Gudrun mittens   16, 54

Rona cardigan   18, 56

Soren sweater   20, 62

Thor cowl   22, 66

Stig cushion   24, 68

Elsa poncho   26, 70

Ebba beret   28, 74

Anders waistcoat   30, 76

Olav mug hug   32, 80

Jorgen slipover   34, 81

Valentin hat   36, 84

Klaus scarf   38, 86

Pine trees bottle tops   40, 88

Ola scarf   42, 90

Useful information/abbreviations   92

Stockists   94

Yarn information/acknowledgments   96

introduction

Ever since my first book (*Nordic Knits*) of mixed small Fairisle and cable designs in Rowan yarns, I have been itching to do another one. And here it is! This time, though, I have changed the emphasis. The first book featured mostly colourwork designs with a few cable and textured patterns; this one is the opposite: mostly cables with a few Fairisle knits.

The projects offer a range of garments and accessories (for women and for men) all in Rowan yarns, as well as some nice things for the home including a big luxurious cable bed runner that doubles as a wrap, in quick-to-knit *Big Wool* and a couple of elegant cabled cushions, one in *Pure Wool Worsted* and the other in *Pure Wool DK*. My Soren sweater, also in *Pure Wool Worsted*, and my Jorgen slipover in *Hemp Tweed* are unisex, with different colourways for men and women. Three handsome scarves with interestingly varied cable designs in *Pure Wool Worsted*, a unisex cable bobble hat in *Hemp Tweed*, two Fairisle hats in *Felted Tweed* and a pair of cable fingerless mittens in luxurious cashmere provide a great collection of accessories.

The big Elsa poncho in *Creative Focus Worsted* with its cowl neck, buttoned sides and big cable panel is a must-have design for her while the subtly coloured Fairisle Anders waistcoat in *Hemp Tweed* makes a great item for him.

I hope you enjoy choosing and knitting the designs in the book as much as I did creating them, with the help of my usual ever-professional team. A special thank you to Penny and Lee, for the use of their house near mine in Ilfracombe as a location and for gamely modelling some of the knits, along with my niece Harriet.

8

rune bed runner

christa hat

frode cushion

thora scarf

gudrun mittens

rona cardigan

soren sweater

thor cowl

stig cushion

elsa poncho

ebba beret

anders waistcoat

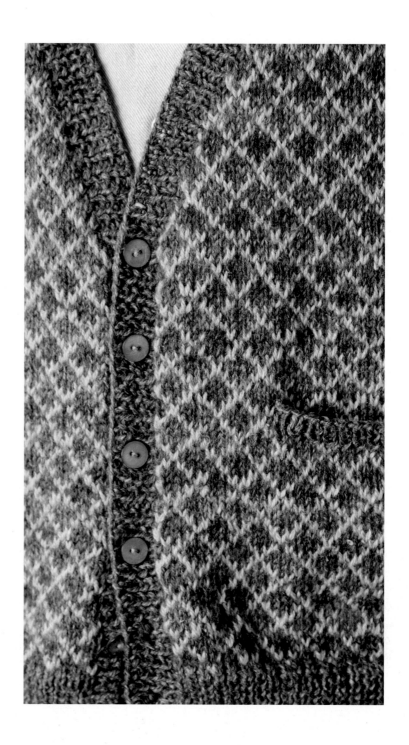

olav mug hug

jorgen slipover

valentin hat

klaus scarf

pine trees bottle tops

ola scarf

rune bed runner

MEASUREMENTS

Approx 100cm/39½in wide by 220cm/86½in long.

YARN

22 x 100g balls of Rowan *Big Wool* Linen 048.

NEEDLES

Pair 10mm (US 15) knitting needles.
Cable needle.

TENSION

9 sts and 12½ rows to 10cm/4in square over st st using 10mm (US 15) needles, or size to obtain correct tension.

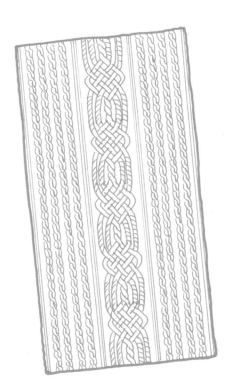

ABBREVIATIONS

C4B Slip next 2 sts onto a cable needle and leave at back of work, k2, then k2 from cable needle.

C4F Slip next 2 sts onto a cable needle and leave at front of work, k2, then k2 from cable needle.

C6B Slip next 3 sts onto a cable needle and leave at back of work, k3, then k3 from cable needle.

C6F Slip next 3 sts onto a cable needle and leave at front of work, k3, then k3 from cable needle.

Cr4R Slip next st onto a cable needle and leave at back of work, k3, then p1 from cable needle.

Cr4L Slip next 3 sts onto a cable needle and leave at front of work, p1, then k3 from cable needle.

T5R Slip next 2 sts onto a cable needle and leave at back of work, k3, then p2 from cable needle.

T5L Slip next 3 sts onto a cable needle and leave at front of work, p2, then k3 from cable needle.

wrap 3 Yrn, p3, then lift the yrn over these 3 sts and off the needle.

See also page 93.

NOTE

When working from Chart, right side rows are read from right to left; wrong side rows are read from left to right.

CENTRE PANEL

Using 10mm (US 15) needles cast on 36 sts.
Row 1 (rs) P1, [p1, k1] twice, p4, [k2, p2] 4 times, k2, p4, [k1, p1] twice, p1.
Row 2 (ws) K1, [k1, p1] twice, k4, p2, [k2, p2] 4 times, k4 [p1, k1] twice, k1.
These 2 rows **set** the patt.
Work a further 3 rows in patt.
Inc row Patt 9, [m1, p1] twice, [k1, m1] twice, p2, [k1, m1, k1, p2] twice, [m1, k1] twice, [p1, m1] twice, patt 9. *46 sts.*
Cont in patt from Chart.

CENTRE PANEL

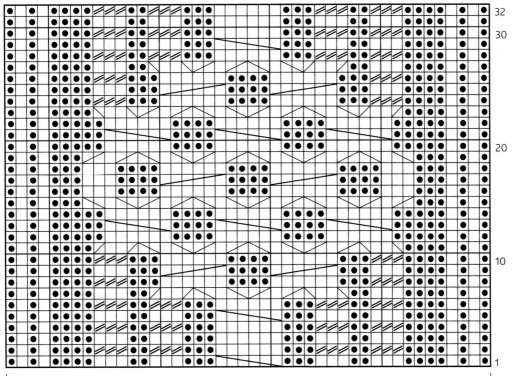

44 sts

LEFT AND RIGHT SIDE PANELS

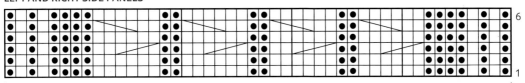

46 sts

KEY

☐ K on RS, P on WS		T5R
⬤ P on RS, K on WS		T5L
	C4B		C6B
	C4F		C6F
	Cr4R		wrap 3
	Cr4L		

Row 1 P1, work row 1 from Chart, p1.

Row 2 K1, work row 2 from Chart, k1.

These 2 rows **set** the Chart with 1 st at sides in rev st st.

Rows 3 to 32 Working correct rows of Chart, work in patt as set.

These 32 rows form the patt rep.

Rep these 32 rows seven times more then row 1 again, ending on a right side row.

Dec row Patt 8, [p2tog] twice, p1, [p2tog] twice, p2, p2tog, p3, p2tog, p2, [p2tog] twice, p1, [p2tog] twice, patt 9. *36 sts.*

Rows 259 to 264 Rep rows 1 and 2 three times.

Cast off in patt.

RIGHT SIDE PANEL

Using 10mm (US 15) needles cast on 35 sts.

Row 1 (rs) K1, [p1, k1] twice, p4, [k2, p2] 4 times, k2, p4, [k1, p1] twice.

Row 2 (ws) [K1, p1] twice, k4, p2 [k2, p2] 4 times, k4, [p1, k1] twice, k1.

These 2 rows **set** the patt

Work a further 3 rows in patt.

Inc row Patt 8, m1, p2, [m1, k1] twice, p1, m1, p1, [k1, m1] twice, p2, [m1, k1] twice, p1, m1, p1, [k1, m1] twice, p2, m1, patt 9. *47 sts.*

Cont in patt from Chart.

Row 1 K1, work row 1 from Chart.

Row 2 Work row 2 from Chart, k1.

These 2 rows **set** the Chart with one st in garter st at right hand edge.

Rows 3 to 6 Working correct rows of Chart, work in patt as set.

Rows 3 to 6 form the 4-row patt.

Rep these 4 rows 62 times more then rows 3 to 5 again, ending on a right side row.

Dec row Patt 7, p2tog, p1, [p2tog] twice, [p1, p2tog] twice, p2tog, p1, p2tog, [p2tog, p1] twice, [p2tog] twice, p1, p2tog, patt 9. *35 sts.*

Rows 259 to 264 Rep rows 1 and 2 three times.

Cast off in patt.

LEFT SIDE PANEL

Using 10mm (US 15) needles cast on 35 sts.

Row 1 (rs) [P1, k1] twice, p4, [k2, p2] 4 times, k2, p4, [k1, p1] twice, k1.

Row 2 (ws) K1, [k1. p1] twice, k4, p2, [k2, p2] 4 times, k4, [p1, k1] twice.

These 2 rows **set** the patt.

Work a further 3 rows in patt.

Inc row Rib 9, m1, p2, [m1, k1] twice, p1, m1, p1, [k1, m1] twice, p2, [m1, k1] twice, p1, m1, p1, [k1, m1] twice, p2, m1, rib 8. *47 sts.*

Cont in patt from Chart.

Row 1 Work row 1 from Chart, k1.

Row 2 K1, work row 2 from Chart.

These 2 rows **set** the Chart with one st in garter st at left hand edge.

Rows 3 to 6 Working correct rows of Chart, work in patt as set.

Rows 3 to 6 form the 4-row patt.

Rep these 4 rows 62 times more, then rows 3 to 5 again, ending on a right side row.

Dec row Patt 9, p2tog, p1, [p2tog] twice, [p1, p2tog] twice, p2tog, p1, p2tog, [p2tog, p1] twice, [p2tog] twice, p1, p2tog, patt 7. *35 sts.*

Rows 259 to 264 Rep rows 1 and 2 three times.

Cast off in patt.

TO MAKE UP

Join row ends of side panels to row ends of centre panel.

christa hat

MEASUREMENTS
To fit an average-size head.

YARN
Rowan *Felted Tweed DK*

1 x 50g ball each of Stone 190 (A), Tawny 186 (B), Seafarer 170 (C), Watery 152 (D), Ginger 154 (E) and Pine 158 (F).

NEEDLES
Pair each 3.25mm (US 3) and 3.75mm (US 5) knitting needles.

TENSION
25 sts and 28 rows to 10cm/4in square over patt st st using 3.75mm (US 5) needles, or size to obtain correct tension.

ABBREVIATIONS
See page 93.

NOTE
When working from Chart odd numbered rows are k rows and read from right to left. Even numbered rows are p rows and read from left to right.

Use the Fairisle method, strand the yarn not in use across the wrong side of work weaving them under and over the working yarn every 3 or 4 sts.

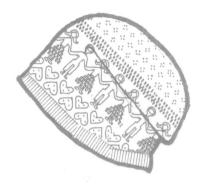

TO MAKE
Using 3.25mm (US 3) needles and F, cast on 106 sts.

Rib row 1 K2, [p2, k2] to end.

Rib row 2 P2, [k2, p2] to end.

These 2 rows form the rib.

Work a further 13 rows.

Row 16 (inc) Rib 3, [m1, rib 2, m1, rib 3] 20 times, m1, rib 3. *147 sts.*

Change to 3.75mm (US 5) needles and work in patt from Chart .

Row 1 K1A, [work across 24-st patt rep of row 1] six times, work one st after patt rep, k1A.

Row 2 P1A, work one st before patt rep, [work across 24-st patt rep of row 2] six times, p1A.

These 2 rows **set** the Chart with one st in st st using A at sides.

Cont in patt to end of row 56.

Cont in A only.

Next row (dec) K4, [k2tog, k1] 46 times, k2tog, k3. *100 sts.*

Next row P to end.

SHAPE CROWN

Row 1 [K7, k2tog] to last st, k1. *89 sts.*

St st 3 rows.

Row 5 [K6, k2tog] to last st, k1. *78 sts.*

St st 3 rows.

Row 9 [K5, k2tog] to last st, k1. *67 sts.*

St st 3 rows.

Row 13 [K4, k2tog] to last st, k1. *56 sts.*

St st 3 rows.

Row 17 [K3, k2tog] to last st, k1. *45 sts.*

St st 1 row.

Row 19 [K2, k2tog] to last st, k1. *34 sts.*

St st 1 row.

Row 21 [K1, k2tog] to last st, k1. *23 sts.*

Row 22 P1, [p2tog] to end. *12 sts.*

Break off yarn, thread through rem
12 sts, draw up and secure.

TO MAKE UP

Join back seam.

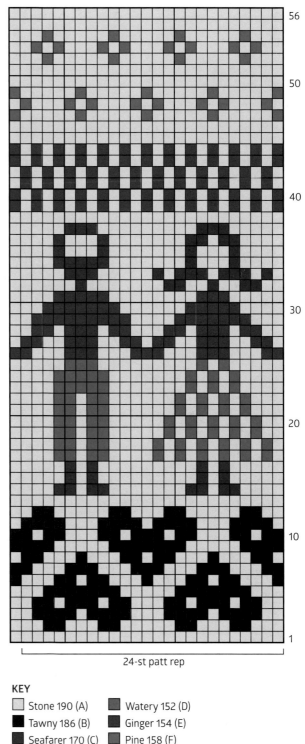

24-st patt rep

KEY

☐ Stone 190 (A) ■ Watery 152 (D)

■ Tawny 186 (B) ■ Ginger 154 (E)

■ Seafarer 170 (C) ■ Pine 158 (F)

frode cushion

MEASUREMENTS

44cm/17¼in square to fit a cushion pad 45cm/17¾in square.

YARN

5 x 50g balls of Rowan *Pure Wool Superwash DK* Flint 105.

NEEDLES

Pair 3.75mm (US 5) knitting needles.
Cable needle.

TENSION

26 sts and 33 rows to 10cm/4in square over patt using 3.75mm (US 5) needles, or size to obtain correct tension.

ABBREVIATIONS

C6B Slip next 3 sts onto a cable needle and leave at back of work, k3, then k3 from cable needle.

Cr3R Slip next st onto a cable needle and leave at back of work, k2, then p1 from cable needle.

Cr3L Slip next 2 sts onto a cable needle and leave at front of work, p1, then k2 from cable needle.

See also page 93.

NOTE

When working from Chart, right side rows are read from right to left; wrong side rows are read from left to right.

BACK AND FRONT (both alike)

Using 3.75mm (US 5) needles cast on 116 sts.

Foundation row (ws) K3, p6, k2, [p1, k6, p2, k2, p2, k2, p1, k2, p6, k2] 4 times, k1.

Work in patt from Chart.

Row 1 (rs) Work one st before patt rep [work across row 1 of 26-st patt rep] 4 times, work 11 sts after patt rep.

Row 2 (ws) Work 11 sts before patt rep [work across row 2 of 26-st patt rep] 4 times, work one st after patt rep.

These 2 rows **set** the 16-row patt rep.

Rep rows 1 to 16 eight times more.

Cast off.

TO MAKE UP

With right sides together, sew back to front along three sides. Insert cushion pad and join rem seam.

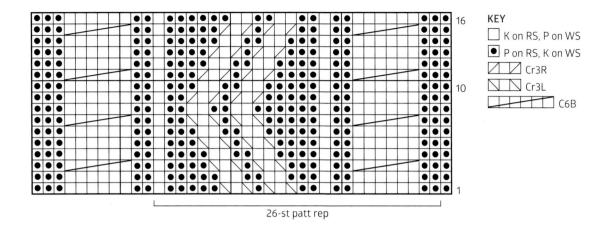

KEY

☐ K on RS, P on WS

● P on RS, K on WS

▨ Cr3R

▨ Cr3L

▨ C6B

16

10

1

26-st patt rep

thora scarf

MEASUREMENTS

Approx 17cm/6in wide, 158cm/62¼in long.

YARN

4 x 100g balls of Rowan *Pure Wool Superwash Worsted*
Lagoon 186
OR
Hawthorn 141.

NEEDLES

Pair of 4.5mm (US 7) knitting needles.
Cable needle.

EXTRAS

2 x large safety pins.

TENSION

20 sts and 25 rows to 10cm/4in square over st st using
4.5mm (US 7) needles, or size to obtain correct tension.

ABBREVIATIONS

C9B Cable 9 back, slip next 5 sts onto a cable needle and
leave at back of work, k4, then k5 from cable needle
C9F Cable 9 front, slip next 4 sts onto a cable needle and
leave at front of work, k5, then k4 from cable needle
See also page 93.

TO MAKE

With 4.5mm (US 7) needles cast on 41 sts.
Row 1 (rs) Sl 1, k to end.
Row 2 As row 1.
Row 3 As row 1.
Row 4 (ws) Sl 1, k9, m1, [k1, m1] twice, K to last 12 sts, m1,
[k1, m1] twice, k10. *47 sts.*
Work in cable knot patt as folls:-
Row 1 (rs) Sl 1, k to end.
Row 2 Sl 1, k7, p9, k13, p9, k8.
Row 3 Sl 1, k7, C9F, k13, C9B, k8.
Rows 4 and 6 As row 2.
Rows 5 and 7 As row 1.
Row 8 As row 2.
Repeat last 8 rows 3 times, then rows 1 and 2 once more.
Row 35 (rs – make cable knot) Sl 1, k5, then leaving these
6 sts on right- hand needle, make first cable strip over next
13 sts as folls:-
* k2, C9F, k2, turn, [k2, p9, k2, turn, k13, turn] 3 times, k2,
p9, k2 *; rep from * to * once more. Break yarn and leave
these 13 sts on first safety pin.
Slip the next 9 sts onto a holder (centre sts). Rejoin yarn to
next stitch then make second cable strip over next 13 sts
as folls:-
* k2, C9B, k2, turn, [k2, p9, k2, turn, k13, turn] 3 times, k2,

p9, k2 *; rep from * to * twice more. Break yarn and leave these 13 sts on a second safety pin.

Ensuring strips are not twisted, now slip sts back onto left-hand needle thus: slip 13 sts from first safety pin (first cable stripe) back onto left-hand needle, then slip the centre 9 sts from holder back onto left-hand needle and by passing them behind those from first cable strip, now wrap the 13 sts on second safety pin (second cable strip) around those of first cable strip by sliding the safety pin, from top to bottom, between the first strip and the centre sts and then bringing it back up level with the other sts, slip these 13 sts back onto left-hand needle, rejoin yarn and work across these 35 sts as folls:- k2, C9B, k13, C9F, k2 (knot completed), then knit the remaining sts on left-hand needle.

Rows 36 and 38 As row 2.

Rows 37 and 39 As row 1.

Row 40 As row 2.

Row 41 As row 1.

Row 42 As row 2.

Row 43 Sl 1, k7, C9B, k13, C9F, k8.

Rows 44 and 46 As row 2.

Rows 45 and 47 As row 1.

Row 48 As row 2.

Repeat last 8 rows 4 times, then rows 41 and 42 once, ending with a wrong side row.

Row 83 (rs – make cable knot) Sl 1, k5, then leaving these 6 sts on right-hand needle, make first cable strip over next 13 sts as folls:-

* k2, C9B, k2, turn, [k2, p9, k2, turn, k13, turn] 3 times, k2, p9, k2 *; rep from * to * once more. Break yarn and leave these 13 sts on first safety pin.

Slip the next 9 sts onto a holder (centre sts). Rejoin yarn to next stitch then make second cable strip over next 13 sts as folls:-

* k2, C9F, k2, turn, [k2, p9, k2, turn, k13, turn] 3 times, k2, p9, k2 *; rep from * to * twice more. Break yarn and leave these 13 sts on a second safety pin.

Ensuring strips are not twisted, now slip sts back onto left-hand needle thus: slip 13 sts from first safety pin (first cable strip) back onto left-hand needle, then slip the centre 9 sts from holder back onto left-hand needle and by passing them behind those from first cable strip, now wrap the 13 sts on second safety pin, (second cable strip) around those of first strip by sliding the safety pin, from top to bottom, between the first strip and the centre sts and then bringing it back up level with the other sts, slip these 13 sts back onto left-hand needle, rejoin yarn and work across these 35 sts as folls:-
k2, C9F, k13, C9B, k2 (knot completed), then knit the remaining sts on left-hand needle.

Rows 84 and 86 As row 2.

Row 85 and 87 As row 1.

Row 88 As row 2.

Row 89 As row 1.

Row 90 As row 2.

Row 91 Sl 1, k7, C9F, k13, C9B, k8.

Rows 92 and 94 As row 2.

Rows 93 and 95 As row 1.

Row 96 As row 2.

These 96 rows **set** the cable knot pattern.

Repeat rows 1 to 96 five more times, then rows 1 to 20 once, ending with a wrong side row. (596 rows of cable knot pattern should have been worked in total).

Next row (rs) K10, [k2tog] 3 times, K to last 16 sts, [k2tog] 3 times, k10. *41 sts.*

Next row K to end.

Next row K to end.

Cast off knitways (on WS).

gudrun mittens

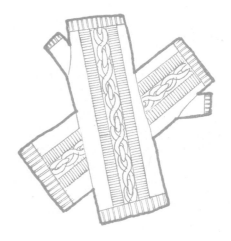

MEASUREMENTS

To fit small/medium hands.

Length 32cm/12½in.

YARN

3 x 25g hanks Rowan *Cashmere* Cream 050.

NEEDLES

Pair each of 4mm (US 6) and 4.5mm (US 7) needles.
Cable needle.

TENSION

20 sts and 28 rows to 10cm (4in) square over st st using
4.5mm (US 7) needles, or size to obtain correct tension.

ABBREVIATIONS

Cr9BF Slip next 6 sts onto a cable needle and leave at back
of work, k3, then slip the last 3 sts on the left of the cable
needle back onto the left hand needle, leave the cable
needle at the front of the work, k3 from left hand needle,
k3 from cable needle.

Cr9FB Slip next 6 sts onto a cable needle and leave at
front of work, k3, then slip the last 3 sts on the left of the
cable needle back onto the left hand needle, leave the
cable needle at the back of the work, k3 from left hand
needle, k3 from cable needle.

See also page 93.

PATTERN PANEL (worked over 15 sts).

Row 1 K15.

Row 2 K3, p9, k3.

Row 3 K3, Cr9FB, k3.

Row 4 K3, p9, k3.

Rows 5 to 10 Rep rows 1 and 2 three times more.

Row 11 K3, Cr9BF, k3.

Row 12 K3, p9, k3.

Rows 13 to 16 Rep rows 1 and 2 twice more.

These 16 rows form the patt and are repeated.

LEFT MITT

With 4mm (US 6) needles cast on 54 sts.

Rib row 1 P2, [k2, p2] to end.

Rib row 2 K2, [p2, k2] to end.

These 2 rows form the rib.

Work a further 9 rows.

Inc row Rib 25, m1pw, rib 14, m1pw, rib 15. *56 sts.*

Change to 4.5mm (US 7) needles.

Row 1 K8, work across row 1 of patt panel, k33.

Row 2 P33, work across row 2 of patt panel, p8.

Row 3 K8, work across row 3 of patt panel, k33.

Row 4 P33, work across row 4 of patt panel, p8.

These 4 rows **set** the patt.

Dec row K3, skpo, patt 21, k2tog, k5, skpo, k16, k2tog, k3. *52 sts.*

Work 9 rows.

Dec row K3, skpo, patt 19, k2tog, k5, skpo, k14, k2tog, k3. *48 sts.*

Work 9 rows.

Dec row K3, skpo, patt 17, k2tog, k5, skpo, k12, k2tog, k3. *44 sts.*

Work 9 rows.

Dec row K3, skpo, patt 15, k2tog, k5, skpo, k10, k2tog, k3. *40 sts.*

Work 9 rows.

** THUMB SHAPING

Row 1 K1, m1, patt to last st, m1, k1.

Row 2 Patt to end.

Row 3 K2, m1, patt to last 2 sts, m1, k2.

Row 4 Patt to end.

Row 5 K3, m1, patt to last 3 sts, m1, k3.

Row 6 Patt to end.

Cont in this way, inc 2 sts on 3rd and every foll 4th row until the foll row has been worked.

Row 25 K8, m1, patt to last 8 sts, m1, k8. *56 sts.*

Row 26 Patt to end.

Row 27 K8, turn.

Beg with a p row work 5 rows st st.

Change to 4mm (US 6) needles.

Rib row 1 K3, p2, k3.

Rib row 2 P3, k2, p3.

Work a further 1 row.

Cast off in rib.

Next row With right side facing and using 4.5mm (US 7) needles, rejoin yarn to next st, patt to end.

Next row P8, turn.

Beg with a k row work 4 rows st st.

Change to 4mm (US 6) needles.

Rib row 1 P3, k2, p3.

Rib row 2 K3, p2, k3.

Work a further 1 row.

Cast off in rib.

Next row With wrong side facing and using 4.5mm (US 7) needles, rejoin yarn to next st, patt to end. *40 sts.*

Work a further 4 rows in patt, dec 2 sts over cable on last row. *38 sts.*

Change to 4mm (US 6) needles.

Rib row 1 P2, [k2, p2] to end.

Rib row 2 K2, [p2, k2] to end.

Work a further 3 rows.

Cast off in rib **.

RIGHT MITT

With 4mm (US 6) needles cast on 54 sts.

Rib row 1 P2, [k2, p2] to end.

Rib row 2 K2, [p2, k2] to end.

These 2 rows form the rib.

Work a further 9 rows.

Inc row Rib 15, m1pw, rib 14, m1pw, rib 25. *56 sts.*

Change to 4.5mm (US 7) needles.

Row 1 K33, work across row 1 of patt panel, k8.

Row 2 P8, work across row 2 of patt panel, p33.

Row 3 K33, work across row 3 of patt panel, k8.

Row 4 P8, work across row 4 of patt panel, p33.

These 4 rows **set** the patt.

Dec row K3, skpo, patt 16, k2tog, k5, skpo, k21, k2tog, k3. *52 sts.*

Work 9 rows.

Dec row K3, skpo, patt 14, k2tog, k5, skpo, k19, k2tog, k3. *48 sts.*

Work 9 rows.

Dec row K3, skpo, patt 12, k2tog, k5, skpo, k17, k2tog, k3. *44 sts.*

Work 9 rows.

Dec row K3, skpo, patt 10, k2tog, k5, skpo, k15, k2tog, k3. *40 sts.*

Work 9 rows.

Now work as given for Left Mitt from ** to **.

TO MAKE UP

Join side and thumb seams.

rona cardigan

MEASUREMENTS

TO FIT BUST

81	86	91	97	102	107	112	cm
32	34	36	38	40	42	44	in

FINISHED MEASUREMENTS

Bust

92	97	102	106	111	116	121	cm
36¼	38	40	41¾	43¾	45½	47½	in

Length to shoulder

53	54	55	56	58	60	61	cm
21	21¼	21½	22	23	23½	24	in

Sleeve length

45cm/17¾in

YARN

5(6:6:7:7:8:8) x 50g balls of Rowan *Felted Tweed DK* Granite 191 (A).

1 x 50g ball each Clay 177 (B) and Pine 158 (C).

2 x 50g balls Bilberry 151 (D).

NEEDLES

Pair each of 3.25mm (US 3) and 3.75mm (US 5) knitting needles.

EXTRAS

8 buttons.

TENSION

25 sts and 25 rows to 10cm/4in square over patt st st using 3.75mm (US 5) needles, or size to obtain correct tension.

ABBREVIATIONS

See page 93.

NOTE

When working from Chart odd numbered rows are k rows and read from right to left. Even numbered rows are p rows and read from left to right.

Use the Fairisle method, strand the yarn not in use across the wrong side of work weaving them under and over the working yarn every 3 or 4 sts.

BACK

Using 3.25mm (US 3) needles and A cast on 114(122:126:134:138:146:150) sts.

1st row K2, [p2, k2] to end.

2nd row P2, [k2, p2] to end.

Rep the last 2 rows 5 times, inc 3(1:3:1:3:1:3) sts across last row. *117(123:129:135:141:147:153) sts.*

Change to 3.75mm (US 5) needles.

Beg with a k row cont in st st and patt from Chart A.

Row 1 Patt 2 sts before patt rep, [work across row 1 of 6-st patt rep] 19(20:21:22:23:24:25) times, patt one st after patt rep.

Row 2 Patt one st before patt rep, [work across row 2 of 6-st patt rep] 19(20:21:22:23:24:25) times, patt 2 sts after patt rep.

These 2 rows **set** the patt.

Rows 3 and 4 Work in patt as set.

Row 5 Using C, k to end, inc 4(6:0:2:4:6:0) sts evenly across row. *121(129:129:137:145:153:153) sts.*

Work in patt from Chart B.

Row 6 [Work across row 1 of 8-st patt rep] 15(16:16:1718:19:19) times, patt one st after patt rep.

Row 7 Patt one st before patt rep, [work across row 2 of 8-st patt rep] 15(16:16:17:18:19:19) times.

These 2 rows **set** the patt.

Rows 8 to 27 Working correct rows of Chart work in patt as set.

Row 28 Using C p to end, dec 4(6:0:2:4:6:0) sts evenly across row. *117(123:129:135:141:147:153) sts.*

Work in patt from Chart C.

Row 29 Patt 2 sts before patt rep, [work across row 1 of 6-st patt rep] 19(20:21:22:23:24:25) times, patt one st after patt rep.

Row 30 Patt one st before patt rep, [work across row 2 of 6-st patt rep] 19(20:21:22:23:24:25) times, patt 2 sts after patt rep.

These 2 rows **set** the patt.

Rows 31 to 42 Working correct rows of Chart work in patt as set.

Now rep rows 5 to 14 of Chart to form main patt.

Work straight until back measures 27(28:28:29:29:30:30) cm/10½(11:11:11½:11½:11¾:11¾)in from cast-on edge, ending with a p row.

SHAPE RAGLAN ARMHOLES

Cast off 4(5:6:7:8:9:10) sts at beg of next 2 rows. *109(113:117:121:125:129:133) sts.*

Next row K2, skpo, k to last 4 sts, k2tog, k2.

Next row P to end.

Next row K to end.

Next row P to end.

Rep the last 4 rows 5 times more. *97(101:105:109:113:117:121) sts.*

CHART A

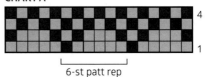

6-st patt rep

CHART B

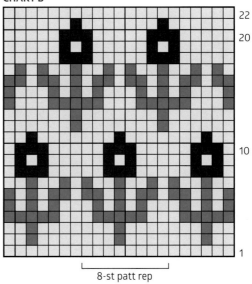

8-st patt rep

CHART C

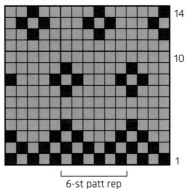

6-st patt rep

KEY

Granite 191 (A)
Clay 177 (B)
Pine 158 (C)
Bilberry 151 (D)

Next row K2, skpo, k to last 4 sts, k2tog, k2.

Next row P to end.

Rep the last 2 rows 12(13:14:15:16:17:18) times more and the first row again. *69(71:73:75:77:79:81) sts.*

Next row P2tog, patt to last 2 sts, p2tog. *67(69:71:73:75:77:79) sts.*

Leave these sts on a holder.

LEFT FRONT

Using 3.25mm (US 3) needles and A cast on 55(59:63:63:67:71:75) sts.

1st row K2, [p2, k2] to last 5 sts, p2, k3.

2nd row P3, [k2, p2] to end.

Rep the last 2 rows 5 times, inc 2(1:0:3:2:1:0) sts evenly across last row. *57(60:63:66:69:72:75) sts.*

Change to 3.75mm (US 5) needles.

Beg with a k row cont in st st and patt from Chart A.

Row 1 Patt one st before patt rep, [work across row 1 of 6-st patt rep] 9(9:10:10:11:11:12) times, patt 2(5:2:5:2:5:2) sts after patt rep.

Row 2 Patt 2(5:2:5:2:5:2) sts before patt rep, [work across row 2 of 6-st patt rep] 9(9:10:10:11:11:12) times, patt one st after patt rep.

These 2 rows **set** the patt.

Rows 3 and 4 Work in patt as set.

Row 5 Using C k to end, inc 4(5:2:3:4:5:2) sts evenly across row. *61(65:65:69:73:77:77) sts.*

Work in patt from Chart B.

Row 6 Patt one st before patt rep, [work across row 1 of 8-st patt rep] 7(8:8:8:9:9:9) times, patt 4(0:0:4:0:4:4) sts after patt rep.

Row 7 Patt 4(0:0:4:0:4:4) sts before patt rep, [work across row 2 of 8-st patt rep] 7(8:8:8:9:9:9) times, patt one st after patt rep.

These 2 rows **set** the patt.

Rows 8 to 27 Working correct rows of Chart work in patt as set.

Row 28 Using C p to end, dec 4(5:2:3:4:5:2) sts evenly across row. *57(60:63:66:69:72:75) sts.*

Work in patt from Chart C.

Row 29 Patt one st before patt rep, [work across row 1 of 6-st patt rep] 9(9:10:10:11:11:12) times, patt 2(5:2:5:2:5:2) sts after patt rep.

Row 30 Patt 2(5:2:5:2:5:2) sts before patt rep, [work across row 2 of 6-st patt rep] 9(9:10:10:11:11:12) times, patt one st after patt rep.

These 2 rows **set** the patt.

Rows 31 to 42 Working correct rows of Chart work in patt as set.

Now rep rows 5 to 14 of Chart to form main patt.

Work straight until front measures 27(28:28:29:29:30:30)cm/ 10½(11:11:11½:11½:11¾:11¾)in from cast-on edge, ending with a p row.

SHAPE RAGLAN ARMHOLE

Next row Cast off 4(5:6:7:8:9:10) sts, patt to end. *53(55:57:59:61:63:65) sts.*

Next row P to end.

Next row K2, skpo, k to end.

Next row P to end.

Next row K to end.

Next row P to end.

Rep the last 4 rows twice more. *50(52:54:56:58:60:62) sts.*

Next row K2, skpo, k to end.

Next row P to end.

Rep the last 2 rows 15(16:17:18:19:20:21) times. *34(35:36:37:38:39:40) sts.*

SHAPE FRONT NECK

Next row K2, skpo, k11, turn and work on these sts for neck shaping, leave rem sts on a holder.

Next row Cast off 2 sts, p to end.

Next row K2, skpo, k to end.

Rep the last 2 rows twice more. *5 sts.*

Next row Cast off 2 sts, p2tog. *2 sts.*

Leave these sts on a holder.

RIGHT FRONT

Using 3.25mm (US 3) needles and A cast on 55(59:63:63:67:71:75) sts.

1st row K3, [p2, k2] to end.

2nd row P2, [k2, p2] to last 5 sts, k2, p3.

Rep the last 2 rows 5 times, inc 2(1:0:3:2:1:0) sts evenly across last row. *57(60:63:66:69:72:75) sts.*

Change to 3.75mm (US 5) needles.

Beg with a k row cont in st st and patt from Chart A.

Row 1 Patt 2(5:2:5:2:5:2) sts before patt rep, [work across row 1 of 6-st patt rep] 9(9:10:10:11:11:12) times, patt one st after patt rep.

Row 2 Patt one st before patt rep, [work across row 2 of 6-st patt rep] 9(9:10:10:11:11:12) times, patt 2(5:2:5:2:5:2) sts after patt rep.

These 2 rows **set** the patt.

Rows 3 and 4 Work in patt as set.

Row 5 Using C k to end, inc 4(5:2:3:4:5:2) sts evenly across row. *61(65:65:69:73:77:77) sts.*

Work in patt from Chart B.

Row 6 Patt 4(0:0:4:0:4:4) sts before patt rep, [work across row 1 of 8-st patt rep] 7(8:8:8:9:9:9) times, patt one st after patt rep.

Row 7 Patt one st before patt rep, [work across row 2 of 8-st patt rep] 7(8:8:8:9:9:9) times, patt 4(0:0:4:0:4:4) sts after patt rep.

These 2 rows **set** the patt.

Rows 8 to 27 Working correct rows of Chart work in patt as set.

Row 28 Using C p to end, dec 4(5:2:3:4:5:2) sts evenly across row. *57(60:63:66:69:72:75) sts.*

Work in patt from Chart C.

Row 29 Patt 2(5:2:5:2:5:2) sts before patt rep, [work across row 1 of 6-st patt rep] 9(9:10:10:11:11:12) times, patt one st after patt rep.

Row 30 Patt one st before patt rep, [work across row 2 of 6-st patt rep] 9(9:10:10:11:11:12) times, patt 2(5:2:5:2:5:2) sts after patt rep.

These 2 rows **set** the patt.

Rows 31 to 42 Working correct rows of Chart work in patt as set.

Now rep rows 5 to 14 of Chart to form main patt.

Work straight until front measures 27(28:28:29:29:30:30) cm/10½(11:11:11½:11½:11¾:11¾)in from cast-on edge, ending with a k row.

SHAPE RAGLAN ARMHOLE

Next row Cast off 4(5:6:7:8:9:10) sts, patt to end. *53(55:57:59:61:63:65) sts.*

Next row K to last 4 sts, k2tog, k2.

Next row P to end.

Next row K to end.

Next row P to end.

Rep the last 4 rows twice more. *50(52:54:56:58:60:62) sts.*

Next row K to last 4 sts, k2tog, k2.

Next row P to end.

Rep the last 2 rows 15(16:17:18:19:20:21) times. *34(35:36:37:38:39:40) sts.*

SHAPE FRONT NECK

Next row K19(20:21:22:23:24:25), leave these sts on a holder, k to last 4 sts, k2tog, k2.

Next row P to end.

Next row Cast off 2 sts, k to last 4 sts, k2tog, k2.

Rep the last 2 rows twice more. 5 sts.

Next row P to end.

Next row Cast off 2 sts, k2tog. 3 sts.

Leave these sts on a holder.

SLEEVES

Using 3.25mm (US 3) needles and A cast on 50(54:58:62:66:70:74) sts.

Rib row 1 K2, [p2, k2] to end.

Rib row 2 P2, [k2, p2] to end.

These 2 rows form the rib.

Work a further 14 rows, inc one st at centre of last row. *51(55:59:63:67:71:75) sts.*

Change to 3.75mm (US 5) needles.

Beg with a k row cont in st st and patt from Chart A.

Row 1 Patt 2(4:6:2:4:6:2) sts before patt rep, [work across row 1 of 6-st patt rep] 8(8:8:10:10:10:12) times, patt 1(3:5:1:3:5:1) sts after patt rep.

Row 2 Patt 1(3:5:1:3:5:1) sts before patt rep, [work across row 2 of 6-st patt rep] 8(8:8:10:10:10:12) times, patt 2(4:6:2:4:6:2) sts after patt rep.

These 2 rows **set** the patt.

Rows 3 and 4 Work in patt as set.

Row 5 Using C k1, m1, k to last st, m1, k1. 53(57:61:65:69:73:77) sts.

Work in patt from Chart B.

Row 6 Patt 2(4:6:0:2:4:6) sts before patt rep [work across row 1 of 8-st patt rep] 6(6:6:8:8:8:8) times, patt 3(5:7:1:3:5:7) sts after patt rep.

Row 7 Patt 3(5:7:1:3:5:7) sts before patt rep, [work across row 2 of 8-st patt rep] 6(6:6:8:8:8:8) times, patt 2(4:6:0:2:4:6) sts after patt rep.

These 2 rows **set** the patt.

Rows 8 to 27 Working correct rows of Chart work in patt as set, increasing one st at each end of rows 11, 17 and 23.

59(63:67:71:75:79:83) sts.

Row 28 Using C p1, m1pw, p to last st, m1pw, p1. *61(65:69:73:77:81:85) sts.*

Work in patt from Chart C.

Row 29 Patt 0(2:4:0:2:4:0) sts before patt rep, [work across row 1 of 6-st patt rep] 10(10:10:12:12:12:14) times, patt 1(3:5:1:3:5:1) sts after patt rep.

Row 30 Patt 1(3:5:1:3:5:1) sts before patt rep, [work across row 2 of 6-st patt rep] 10(10:10:12:12:12:14) times, patt 0(2:4:0:2:4:0) sts after patt rep.

These 2 rows **set** the patt.

Rows 31 to 42 Working correct rows of Chart work in patt as set, increasing one st at each end of rows 35 and 41.

65(69:73:77:81:85:89) sts.

Now rep rows 5 to 14 of Chart to form main patt. **At the same time** inc and work into patt one st at each end of 5th and every foll 8th row until there are *77(81:85:89:93:97:101) sts.*

Cont straight until Sleeve measures

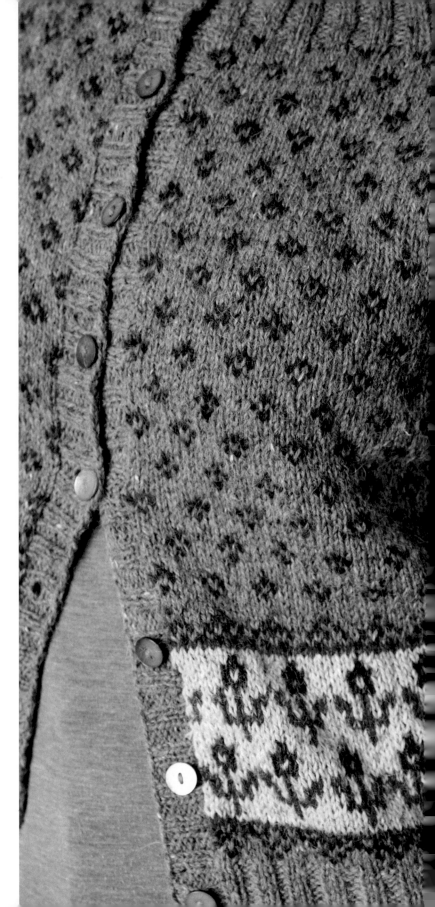

45cm/17¾in from cast-on edge, ending with a
p row.

SHAPE RAGLAN TOP
Cast off 4(5:6:7:8:9:10) sts at beg of next 2 rows.
69(71:73:75:77:79:81) sts.
Next row K2, skpo, k to last 4 sts, k2tog, k2.
Next row P to end.
Next row K to end.
Next row P to end.
Rep the last 4 rows twice more. *63(65:67:69:71:73:75) sts.*
Next row K2, skpo, k to last 4 sts, k2tog, k2.
Next row P to end.
Rep the last 2 rows 18(19:20:21:22:23:24) times, then the
first of these 2 rows again. *23 sts.*
Next row P2tog, patt to last 2 sts, p2tog. *21 sts.*
Leave these sts on a holder.

NECKBAND

With right side facing, using 3.25mm (US 3) needles and
A, k19(20:21:22:23:24:25) from front neck holder, pick up
and k8 sts up right side of front neck, k2 from holder, k21
across right sleeve, k67(69:71:73:75:77:79) from back neck
holder, k21 across left sleeve, k2 from holder, pick up and
k9 sts down left side of front neck, k19(20:21:22:23:24:25)
from left front holder. *168(172:176:180:184:188:192) sts.*
Row 1 P3, [k2, p2] to last 5 sts, k2, p3.
Row 2 K3, [p2, k2] to last 5 sts, p2, k3.
Rep the last 2 rows 3 times more and the first row again.
Cast off in rib.

BUTTONBAND

With 3.25mm (US 3) needles and A, pick up and
k106(110:114:118:122:126:130) sts along left front edge.
Rib row 1 P2, [k2, p2] to end.
Rib row 2 K2, [p2, k2] to end.
Rep the last 2 rows twice more and row 1 again.
Cast off in rib.

BUTTONHOLE BAND

With 3.25mm (US 3) needles and A, pick up and
k106(110:114:118:122:126:130) sts along right front edge,
Rib row 1 P2, [k2, p2] to end.
Rib row 2 K2, [p2, k2] to end.
Rib row 3 P2, [k2, p2] to end.
Buttonhole row Rib 3(3:3:3:4:4:4), [rib 2tog, yf,
rib 12(13:13:14:14:15:15), rib 2tog, rib 12(12:13:13:14:14:15)]
3 times, rib 2tog, rib 12(13:13:14:14:15:15), rib 2tog,
yf, rib 3(3:4:4:4:4:5).
Work 3 rows in rib.
Cast off in rib.

TO MAKE UP

Join raglan and seams. Join side and sleeve seams. Sew on
buttons.

soren sweater

MEASUREMENTS

TO FIT BUST

81	86	91	97	102	107	cm
32	34	36	38	40	42	in

FINISHED MEASUREMENTS

Bust/Chest

98	104	110	116	122	128	cm
38½	41	43¼	45½	48	50½	in

Her length to shoulder

65	66	67	68	69	70	cm
25½	26	26½	26¾	27¼	27½	in

His length to shoulder

68	69	70	71	72	73	cm
26¾	27¼	27½	28	28½	28¾	in

Her sleeve length

45cm/17¾in

His sleeve length

50cm/19¾in

YARN

Rowan *Pure Wool Superwash Worsted*.

Her version

4(4:4:5:5:5) x 100g balls Soft Cream 102 (A).

2(2:2:3:3:3) x 100g balls Moonstone 112 (B).

His version

4(4:4:5:5:5) x 100g balls Moonstone 112 (A).

2(2:2:3:3:3) x 100g balls Charcoal Grey 155 (B).

NEEDLES

Pair each 4mm (US 6) and 4.5mm (US 7) knitting needles.

TENSION

20 sts and 25 rows to 10cm/4in square over st st on 4.5mm (US 7) needles, or size to obtain correct tension.

ABBREVIATIONS

See page 93.

NOTE

When working from Chart, right side rows are k rows and read from right to left; wrong side rows are p rows and read from left to right.

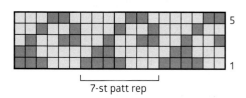

7-st patt rep

KEY

☐ Colour A

■ Colour B

BACK

With 4mm (US 6) needles and B, cast on 99(105:111:117:123:129) sts.

Rib row 1 K1, [p1, k1] to end.

Rib row 2 P1, [k1, p1] to end.

Rep the last 2 rows 9 times more.

Change to 4.5mm (US 7) needles.

Beg with a k row, cont in st st.

Work 30(32:34:36:38:40) rows.

Work in patt from Chart.

Row 1 Patt 4(0:3:6:2:5) sts before patt rep, [work across row 1 of 7-st patt rep] 13(15:15:15:17:17) times, patt 4(0:3:6:2:5) sts after patt rep.

Row 2 Patt 4(0:3:6:2:5) sts before patt rep, [work across row 2 of 7 st patt rep] 13(15:15:15:17:17) times, patt 4(0:3:6:2:5) sts after patt rep.

These 2 rows **set** the Chart.

Work a further 3 rows.

Cont in A only.

Work straight until Back measures 40cm/15¾in from cast-on edge, ending with a p row.

HER VERSION

Shape raglan armholes

Cast off 4(5:6:7:8:9) sts at beg of next 2 rows. *91(95:99:103:107:111) sts.*

Next row K2, skpo, k to last 4 sts, k2tog, k2.

Next row P2, p2tog, p to last 4 sts, p2tog tbl, p2.

Rep the last 2 rows 3 times more. *75(79:83:87:91:95) sts.*

Next row K2, skpo, k to last 4 sts, k2tog, k2.

Next row P to end.

Rep the last 2 rows 21(22:23:24:25:26) times.

Leave rem 31(33:35:37:39:41) sts on a holder.

HIS VERSION

Shape raglan armholes

Cast off 4(5:6:7:8:9) sts at beg of next 2 rows. *91(95:99:103:107:111) sts.*

Next row K2, skpo, k to last 4 sts, k2tog, k2.

Next row P to end.

Rep the last 2 rows 29(30:31:32:33:34) times.

Leave rem 31(33:35:37:39:41) sts on a holder.

FRONT

BOTH VERSIONS

Work as given for back until 43(45:47:49:51:53) sts rem, ending with a wrong side row.

Shape front neck

Next row K2, skpo, k8, skpo, turn and work on these 12 sts for first side of front neck.

Next row P to end.

Next row K2, skpo, k to last 2 sts, skpo.

Next row P to end.

Rep the last 2 rows 3 times more. *4 sts.*

Next row K2, skpo.

Next row P3.

Leave these sts on a holder.

With right side facing, slip centre 15(17:19:21:23:25) sts onto a holder, rejoin yarn to rem sts, k2tog, k to last 4 sts, k2tog, k2.

Next row P to end.

Next row K2tog, k to last 4 sts, k2tog, k2.

Next row P to end.

Rep the last 2 rows 3 times more. *4 sts.*

Next row K2tog, k2.

Next row P3.

Leave these sts on a holder.

SLEEVES

With 4mm (US 6) needles and B, cast on 50(54:58:62:66:72) sts.

Rib row [K1, p1] to end.

Work a further 19 rows, inc one st at centre of last row. *51(55:59:63:67:73) sts.*

Change to 4.5mm (US 7) needles.

Beg with a k row cont in st st.

Work 6 rows.

Inc row K3, m1, k to last 3 sts, m1, k3.

Work 5 rows.

Rep the last 6 rows twice and the inc row again. *59(63:67:71:75:81) sts.*

Work in patt from Chart – noting the first row will be a p row.

Row 1 Patt 5(0:2:4:6:2) sts before patt rep, [work across row 1 of 7-st patt rep] 7(9:9:9:9:11) times, patt 5(0:2:4:6:2) sts after patt rep.

Row 2 Patt 5(0:2:4:6:2) sts before patt rep, [work across row 2 of 7-st patt rep] 7(9:9:9:9:11) times, patt 5(0:2:4:6:2) sts after patt rep.

These 2 rows **set** the Chart.

Work a further 3 rows.

Cont in A only.

HER VERSION

Inc row K3, m1, k to last 3 sts, m1, k3.

Work 5 rows.

Rep the last 6 rows 7 times and the inc row again. *77(81:85:89:93:99) sts.*

Cont straight until Sleeve measures 45cm/17¾in from cast on edge, ending with a wrong side row.

Shape sleeve top

Cast off 4(5:6:7:8:9) sts at beg of next 2 rows. *69(71:73:75:77:81) sts.*

Next row K2, skpo, k to last 4 sts, k2tog, k2.

Next row P to end.

Rep the last 2 rows 25(26:27:28:29:30) times.

Leave rem 17(17:17:17:19:21) sts on a holder.

HIS VERSION

Inc row K3, m1, k to last 3 sts, m1, k3.

Work 7 rows.

Rep the last 8 rows 7 times and the inc row again. *77(81:85:89:93:99) sts.*

Cont straight until Sleeve measures 50cm/19¾in from cast-on edge, ending with a wrong side row.

Shape sleeve top

Cast off 4(5:6:7:8:9) sts at beg of next 2 rows. *69(71:73:75:77:81) sts.*

Next row K2, skpo, k to last 4 sts, k2tog, k2.

Next row P to end.

Next row K to end.

Next row P to end.

Rep the last 4 rows 3 times. *61(63:65:67:69:73) sts.*

Next row K2, skpo, k to last 4 sts, k2tog, k2.

Next row P to end.

Rep the last 2 rows 21(22:23:24:25:26) times.

Leave rem 17(17:17:17:17:19) sts on a holder.

NECKBAND

Join both front and right back raglan seams.

With right side facing, using 4mm (US 6) needles and A, k16(16:16:16:16:18) sts from left sleeve, k last st tog with first st on holder, k2, pick up and k12 sts down left side of front neck, k15(17:19:21:23:25) sts from centre front holder, pick up and k11 sts up right side of front neck, k2, on holder k last st tog with first st on right sleeve, k15(15:15:15:15:17) sts from right sleeve, k last st tog with first st on back, k30(32:34:36:38:40). *106(110:114:118:122:130) sts.*

Rib row [K1, p1] to end.

Work a further 9 rows.

Cast off in rib.

TO MAKE UP

Join left back raglan and neckband seam. Join side and sleeve seams.

thor cowl

MEASUREMENTS

74cm/29¼in circumference; 41cm/16in deep.

YARN

4 x 50g balls of Rowan *Hemp Tweed* Pumice 138.

NEEDLES

4mm (US 6) and 4.5mm (US 7) circular knitting needles,
60cm long.
Cable needle.

TENSION

19 sts and 25 rows to 10cm/4in square over st st using
4.5mm (US 7) needles, or size to obtain correct tension.

ABBREVIATIONS

C6B Slip next 3 sts onto a cable needle and leave at back
of work, k3, then k3 from cable needle.

C6F Slip next 3 sts onto a cable needle and leave at front
of work, k3, then k3 from cable needle.

Cr5R Slip next 2 sts onto a cable needle and leave at back
of work, k3, then p2 from cable needle.

Cr5L Slip next 3 sts onto a cable needle and leave at front
of work, p2, then k3 from cable needle.

See also page 93.

NOTE

When working from Chart all rows are right side rows and
read from right to left.

TO MAKE

Using 4mm (US 6) circular needle cast on 216 sts.
Taking care not to twist the sts, work in rounds as folls:
Round 1 [K2, p2] to end.
Place a marker between first and last st of last round to
denote beg and end of round.

Rep this round 6 times more.
Round 8 (inc) [Rib 2, m1, rib 43, m1, rib 27] 3 times.
222 sts.
Change to 4.5mm (US 7) circular needle and work in patt
from Chart.
Round 9 [Work across round 1 of 74-st patt rep] 3 times.
This round **sets** the patt.
Work in patt to end of round 16.
Rounds 9 to 16 form the 8-round patt rep.
Rep rounds 9 to 16 ten times more, then round 9 again.
Change to 4mm (US 6) circular needle.
Round 98 (dec) * K1, k2tog, [p2, k2] 10 times, p2, k1, k2tog,
[p2, k2] 6 times, p2; rep from * twice more. *216 sts*.
Round 99 [K2, p2] to end.
Rep this round 5 times more.
Cast off in rib.

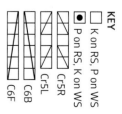

KEY
□ K on RS, P on WS
● P on RS, K on WS

C6F
C6B
Cr5L
Cr5R

stig cushion

MEASUREMENTS

40cm/16in square to fit a cushion pad 40cm/16in.

YARN

4 x 100g balls of Rowan *Pure Wool Superwash Worsted* Moonstone 112.

NEEDLES

Pair of 4.5mm (US 7) knitting needles.

EXTRAS

Beads

Debbie Abrahams – Size 6 x 96 beads.

TENSION

20 sts and 25 rows to 10cm/4in square over st st using 4.5mm (US 7) needles, or size to obtain correct tension.

ABBREVIATIONS

Sl1 wyib Slip one stitch purlwise with yarn at back of work (**WS** of work).

Sl1 wyif Slip one stitch purlwise with yarn in front of work (**WS** of work).

Cr5 Drop first slip stitch off needle to front of work, slip next 3 sts, drop second slip stitch off needle to front: then holding the 3 knit sts on right hand needle, pick up the first dropped st onto left hand needle: then slip the 3 sts back to left hand needle: then with point of right hand needle, pick up the second dropped st and place it on left hand needle: then k5.

place bead On WS rows – place bead by taking yarn to RS of work, slipping bead up next to stitch just worked, slip next stitch purlways from left needle to right needle and bring yarn back to **WS**, leaving bead sitting in front of slipped stitch.

See also page 93.

Special Note for Beads

Before starting to knit, thread beads onto yarn. To do this, thread a fine sewing needle [one that will easily pass through the beads] with sewing thread. Knot ends of thread and then pass end of yarn through this loop. Thread a bead onto sewing thread and gently slide it along and onto knitting yarn. Continue in this way until required number of beads are on yarn.

NOTE

When working from Chart odd numbered rows are read from right to left. Even numbered rows are read from left to right.

FRONT

Thread on 96 Beads – see **Special Note for Beads**

With 4.5mm (US7) needles cast on 86 sts.

Row 1 (rs) K52, [p1, k3] 8 times, p2.

Row 2 K2, [p1, m1p, p1, m1p, p1, k1] 8 times, p52. *102 sts.*

Work in patt from Chart.

Row 1 K52, [work across row 1 of 6-st patt rep] 8 times, work 2 sts after patt rep.

Row 2 Work 2 sts before patt rep, [work across row 2 of 6-st patt rep] 8 times, p52.

These 2 rows **set** the chart and st st for the 8-row patt rep.

Cont in patt for a further 98 rows.

Row 103 (rs) K52, [p1, k2tog, k1, k2tog] 8 times, p2. *86 sts.*

Row 104 P2, [k1, p3] 8 times, p52.

Cast off in patt.

BACK

With 4.5mm (US 7) needles cast on 85 sts.

Beg with a K row, cont in st st for 104 rows.

Cast off.

TO MAKE UP

With right sides together, sew back to front along 3 sides.

Insert cushion pad, join rem seam.

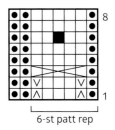

6-st patt rep

KEY

☐ K on RS, P on WS

● P on RS, K on WS

Λ Sl1 wyib

V Sl1 wyif

■ place bead

▭▭▭▭ Cr5

elsa poncho

MEASUREMENTS

Side to side 95cm/37½in.
Length 78cm/30¾in.

YARN

10 x 100g balls Rowan *Creative Focus Worsted* Nickel
00401
OR
10 x 100g balls Rowan *Pure Wool Superwash Worsted*
Moonstone 112.

NEEDLES

Pair each 4.5mm (US 7) and 5mm (US 8) needles.
Circular 4.5mm (US 7) and 5mm (US 8) needle.
Cable needle.

EXTRAS

2 buttons.

TENSION

20 sts and 24 rows to 10cm/4in square over st st using
5mm (US 8) needles, or size to obtain correct tension.
Patt panel (76 sts) measures 26cm/10¼in across and one
patt repeat (28 rows) measures 10cm/4in using 5mm
(US 8) needles, or size to obtain correct tension.

ABBREVIATIONS

C8B Slip next 4 sts onto a cable needle and leave at back
of work, k4 then k4 from cable needle
C8F Slip next 4 sts onto a cable needle and leave at front
of work, k4 then k4 from cable needle
Cr8R Slip next 2 stitches onto a cable needle and hold at
back of work, k6, then p2 from cable needle
Cr8L Slip next 6 sts onto a cable needle and hold at front
of work, p2, then k6 from cable needle
C12B Slip next 6 sts onto a cable needle and hold at back
of work, k6 then k6 from cable needle
C12F Slip next 6 sts onto a cable needle and leave at front
of work, k6 then k6 from cable needle
wrap 1 On a k row, ytf, Sl1, ytb, place slipped st back on
left hand needle; on a p row, ytb, Sl1, ytf, place slipped st
back on left hand needle.
See also page 93.

NOTE

When working from Chart, right side rows are read from
right to left; wrong side rows from left to right.

BACK

CENTRE BACK PANEL

Using 4.5mm (US 7) needles cast on 59 sts.

Moss st row K1, [p1, k1] to end.

Rep this row 14 times more.

Inc row P4, [m1, k1] 5 times, k2, p4, k6, p6, turn, cast on 7 sts, turn, k5, p6, k6, p4, k2, [m1, k1] 5 times, p4. *76 sts.*

Change to 5mm (US 8) needles and work from Chart.

Row 1 P4, k12, p4, k6, p6, k12, p6, k6, p4, k12, p4.

Row 2 K4, p12, k4, p6, k6, p12, k6, p6, k4, p12, k4.

These 2 rows **set** the 56-row patt rep.

Starting at row 3 continue in patt for a further 204 rows, ending with row 38.

Next row P4, [k2tog] twice, slip next 4 sts onto a cable needle and leave at front of work, [slip next st on cable needle, k next st on left hand needle, psso] 4 times, p4, slip next 6 sts onto a cable needle and leave at back of work, [k first st on cable needle tog with first st on left hand needle] 6 times, p12, slip next 6 sts onto a cable needle and leave at front of work, [slip next st on cable needle, k next st on left hand needle, psso] 6 times, p4, [k2tog] twice, slip next 4 sts onto a cable needle and leave at front of work, [slip next st on cable needle, k next st on left hand needle, psso] 4 times, p4. *52 sts.*

Leave these sts on a holder.

BACK RIGHT SIDE PANEL

Using 4.5mm (US 7) needles cast on 73 sts.

Moss st row K1, [p1, k1] to end.

Rep this row 15 times more.

Change to 5mm (US 8) needles.

Row 1 [K1, p1] 5 times, k to end.

Row 2 P to last 9 sts, k1, [p1, k1] 4 times.

These 2 rows **set** the st st with 10 sts in moss st.

Work a further 165 rows, ending at front edge.

Shape upper arm

Next 2 rows P to last 20 sts, wrap 1, turn, k to end.

Next 2 rows P to last 30 sts, wrap 1, turn, k to end.

Next 2 rows P to last 40 sts, wrap 1, turn, k to end.

Next 2 rows P to last 50 sts, wrap 1, turn, k to end.

Next 2 rows P to last 60 sts, wrap 1, turn, k to end.

Leave these 73 sts on a spare needle.

BACK LEFT SIDE PANEL

Using 4.5mm (US 7) needles cast on 73 sts.

Moss st row K1, [p1, k1] to end.

Rep this row 15 times more.

Change to 5mm (US 8) needles.

Row 1 K to last 10 sts, [p1, k1] 5 times.

Row 2 [K1, p1] 4 times, k1, p to end.

These 2 rows **set** the st st with 10 sts in moss st.

Work a further 166 rows, ending at front edge.

Shape upper arm

Next 2 rows K to last 20 sts, wrap 1, turn, p to end.

Next 2 rows K to last 30 sts, wrap 1, turn, p to end.

Next 2 rows K to last 40 sts, wrap 1, turn, p to end.

Next 2 rows K to last 50 sts, wrap 1, turn, p to end.

Next 2 rows K to last 60 sts, wrap 1, turn, p to end.

Leave these 73 sts on a spare needle.

FRONT

CENTRE PANEL

Using 4.5mm (US 7) needles cast on 59 sts.

Moss st row K1, [p1, k1] to end.

Rep this row 14 times more.

Inc row P4, [m1, k1] 5 times, k2, p4, k6, p6, turn, cast on 7 sts, turn, k5, p6, k6, p4, k2, [m1, k1] 5 times, p4. *76 sts.*

Change to 5mm (US 8) needles and work from Chart.

Row 1 P4, k12, p4, k6, p6, k12, p6, k6, p4, k12, p4.

Row 2 K4, p12, k4, p6, k6, p12, k6, p6, k4, p12, k4.

These 2 rows **set** the 56-row patt rep.

Starting at row 3 continue in patt for a further 168 rows, ending with row 2.

Shape neck

Next row Patt 17, turn and work on these sts for first side of front neck.

Next row Cast off 2 sts, patt to end.

Next row Patt to last 2 sts, work 2 tog.

Next row Patt to end.

Rep the last 2 rows 11 times, then work the first of these 2 rows again. *2 sts.*

Cast off.

With right side facing ,rejoin yarn to rem sts, p3, k6, p6, slip next 6 sts onto a cable needle and leave at back of work, [k first st on cable needle tog with first st on left hand needle] 6 times, p6, k6, p3, leave these 36 sts on a holder, cast off next 2 sts, patt to end. *15 sts.*

Next row Patt to end.

Next row Work 2tog, patt to end.

Rep the last 2 rows 12 times. *2 sts.*

Cast off.

FRONT LEFT SIDE PANEL

Using 4.5mm (US 7) needles cast on 73 sts.

Moss st row K1, [p1, k1] to end.

Rep this row 15 times more.

Change to 5mm (US 8) needles.

Row 1 [K1, p1] 5 times, k to end.

Row 2 P to last 9 sts, k1, [p1, k1] 4 times.

These 2 rows **set** the st st with 10 sts in moss st.

Work a further 165 rows, ending at front edge.

Place a marker at beg of last row.

Shape upper arm

Next 2 rows P to last 20 sts, wrap 1, turn, k to end.

Next 2 rows P to last 30 sts, wrap 1, turn, k to end.

Next 2 rows P to last 40 sts, wrap 1, turn, k to end.

Next 2 rows P to last 50 sts, wrap 1, turn, k to end.

Next 2 rows P to last 60 sts, wrap 1, turn, k to end.

Leave these 73 sts on a spare needle.

FRONT RIGHT SIDE PANEL

Using 4.5mm (US 7) needles cast on 73 sts.

Moss st row K1, [p1, k1] to end.

Rep this row 15 times more.

Change to 5mm (US 8) needles.

Row 1 K to last 10 sts, [p1, k1] 5 times.

Row 2 [K1, p1] 4 times, k1, p to end.

These 2 rows **set** the st st with 10 sts in moss st.

Work a further 166 rows, ending at front edge.

Place a marker at beg of last row.

Shape upper arm

Next 2 rows K to last 20 sts, wrap 1, turn, p to end.

Next 2 rows K to last 30 sts, wrap 1, turn, p to end.

Next 2 rows K to last 40 sts, wrap 1, turn, p to end.

Next 2 rows K to last 50 sts, wrap 1, turn, p to end.

Next 2 rows K to last 60 sts, wrap 1, turn, p to end.

Leave these 73 sts on a spare needle.

COLLAR

Join centre front panel to side panels between cast-on edge and coloured threads.

With right side facing, using a 4.5mm (US 7) circular needle pick up and k8 sts along row ends of left front panel, 20 sts down left front neck, k36 from front neck, pick up and k20 sts up right side of front neck, 8 sts along row ends of right front panel, dec one st at centre, k52 sts from back centre panel. *143 sts.*

Rib row 1 K2, [p1, k2] to end.

Rib row 2 P2, [k1, p2] to end.

Rep the last 2 rows 11 times more.

Inc row K2, [p1, m1p, k2] to end. *190 sts.*

Next row P2, [k2, p2] to end.

Work a further 22 rows with rib as now set.

Change to 5mm (US 8) needles.

Work a further 12 rows.

Cast off loosely in rib.

TO MAKE UP

Join centre back panel to side panels. Join shoulder seams. Secure sides together by sewing side borders together with 2 buttons approx 31cm/12in down from shoulder seam.

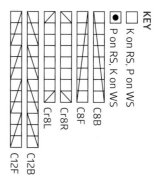

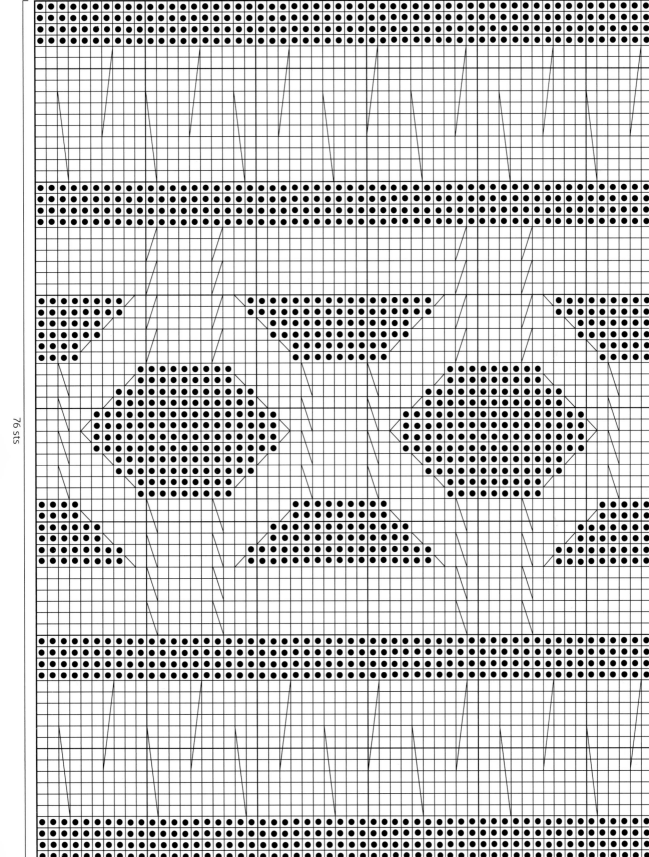

76 sts

1 10 20 30 40 50 56

ebba beret

MEASUREMENTS

To fit an average-size woman's head.

YARN

Rowan *Felted Tweed DK*.

1 x 50g ball each of Stone 190 (A), Bilberry 151 (B), Ginger 154 (C), and Seafarer 170 (D).

NEEDLES

Pair each of 3.25mm (US 3) and 3.75mm (US 5) knitting needles.

TENSION

25 sts and 28 rows to 10cm/4in square over patt st st using 3.75mm (US 5) needles, or size to obtain correct tension.

ABBREVIATIONS

See page 93.

NOTE

When working from Chart, right side rows are k rows and read from right to left; wrong side rows are p rows and read from left to right. Use a combination of Fairisle and Intarsia methods when working the Charts.

TO MAKE

Using 3.25mm (US 3) needles and D, cast on 94 sts.

Rib row 1 K2, [p2, k2] to end.

Rib row 2 P2, [k2, p2] to end.

These 2 rows form the rib.

Work a further 11 rows.

Row 14 (inc) Rib 3, [m1, rib 2, m1, rib 1] 28 times, m1, rib 2, m1, rib 5. *152 sts.*

Change to 3.75 (US 5) needles and work in patt.

Row 1 K [1B, 1A] to end.

Row 2 Using B, p to end.

Row 3 Using A, k to end, inc 3 sts, evenly. *155 sts.*

Work in patt from Chart A.

Row 4 P1A, [work across row 1 of 17-st patt rep] 9 times, p1A.

Row 5 K1A, [work across row 2 of 17-st patt rep] 9 times, k1A,

These 2 rows **set** the chart with one st in st st using A at sides.

Cont in patt to end of row 8.

Row 9 Using A, k to end dec 3 sts evenly across row. *152 sts.*

Work in patt from Chart B.

Row 10 P1A, [work across row 1 of 30-st patt rep] 5 times, 91A.

Row 11 K1A, [work across row 2 of 30-st patt rep] 5 times, k1A,

These 2 rows **set** the chart.

Cont in patt to end of row 30.

Row 31 Using A k to end, inc 3 sts, evenly. *155 sts.*

Rows 32 to 37 As rows 4 to 9 working in patt from Chart A. *152 sts.*

Cont in D only.

Next row P to end.

SHAPE TOP

Row 1 K1, [k13, k2tog] 10 times, k1. *142 sts.*

Row 2 and every foll wrong side row
P to end.

Row 3 K1, [k12, k2tog] 10 times, k1.
132 sts.

Row 5 K1, [k11, k2tog] 10 times, k1.
122 sts.

Row 7 K1, [k10, k2tog] 10 times, k1.
112 sts.

Row 9 K1, [k9, k2tog] 10 times, k1.
102 sts.

Row 11 K1, [k8, k2tog] 10 times, k1.
92 sts.

Row 13 K1, [k7, k2tog] 10 times, k1.
82 sts.

Row 15 K1, [k6, k2tog] 10 times, k1.
72 sts.

Row 17 K1, [k5, k2tog] 10 times, k1.
62 sts.

Row 19 K1, [k4, k2tog] 10 times, k1.
52 sts

Row 21 K1, [k3, k2tog] 10 times, k1.
42 sts.

Row 23 K1, [k2, k2tog] 10 times, k1.
32 sts.

Row 25 K1, [k1, k2tog] 10 times, k1.
22 sts.

Row 27 K1, [k2tog] 10 times, k1.
12 sts.

Row 29 [K2tog] 6 times. 6 sts
Break off yarn, thread through rem 6
sts, draw up and secure.

TO MAKE UP
Join seam.

CHART A

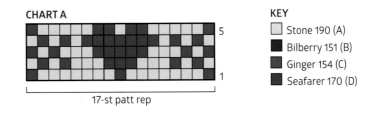

17-st patt rep

KEY
☐ Stone 190 (A)
■ Bilberry 151 (B)
■ Ginger 154 (C)
■ Seafarer 170 (D)

CHART B

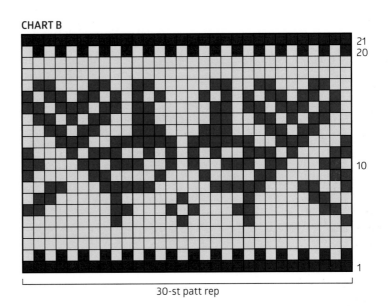

30-st patt rep

anders waistcoat

FINISHED SIZE

TO FIT CHEST

86–91	97–102	107–112	cm
34–36	38–40	42–44	in

ACTUAL MEASUREMENTS

Chest

110	121	131	cm
43¼	47½	51½	in

Length to shoulder

62	64	66	cm
24½	25¼	26	in

YARN

4(4:5) x 50g balls of Rowan *Hemp Tweed* in Pumice 138 (A).
2(2:3) balls each Plum 132 (B), Granite 136 (C) and Treacle
134 (D).

NEEDLES

Pair each of 4mm (US 6) and 4.5mm (US 7) knitting
needles.

EXTRAS

6 buttons.

TENSION

19 sts and 25 rows to 10cm/4in square over st st on 4.5mm
(US 7) needles, or size to obtain correct tension.
24 sts and 24 rows to 10cm/4in square over patt st st on
4.5mm (US 7) needles, or size to obtain correct tension.

ABBREVIATIONS

See page 93.

NOTE

When working from Chart odd numbered rows are k rows
and read from right to left. Even numbered rows are p rows
and read from left to right.
Use the Fairisle method, strand the yarn not in use across
the wrong side of work weaving them under and over the
working yarn every 3 or 4 sts.

BACK

With 4mm (US 6) needles and D, cast on 135(147:159) sts.
Rib row 1 K1, [p1, k1] to end.
Rib row 2 P1, [k1, p1] to end.
These 2 rows form the rib.
Work a further 10 rows.
Change to 4.5mm (US 7) needle and work in patt from
Chart.
Row 1 Work one st before patt rep, [work across row 1 of
6-st patt rep] 22(24:26) times, work 2 sts after patt rep.
Row 2 Work 2 sts before patt rep, [work across row 2 of
6-st patt rep] 22(24:26) times, work one st after patt rep.
These 2 rows **set** the chart for the 24 row patt.
Cont in patt until back measures 39(40:41)cm/15½(15¾:16)in
from cast on edge, ending with a wrong side row.

SHAPE ARMHOLES

Cast off 9(10:11) sts at beg of next 2 rows. *117(127:137) sts.*

Dec one st at each end of the next 6(8:10) rows then 6 foll right side rows. *93(99:105) sts.*

Work straight until back measures 62(64:66)cm/ 24½(25¼: 26)in from cast-on edge, ending with a wrong side row.

Shape shoulders and back neck

Cast off 9 sts at beg of next 2 rows. *75 (81:87) sts*

Next row Cast off 9(10:11) sts, patt until there are 13(14:15) sts on the needle, turn and work on these sts for first side of neck.

Next row Cast off 4 sts, patt to end.

Cast off rem 9(10:11) sts.

With right side facing, return to rem sts, rejoin yarns, cast off centre 31(33:35) sts, patt to end.

Next row Cast off 9(10:11) sts, patt to end.

Next row Cast off 4 sts, patt to end.

Cast off rem 9(10:11) sts.

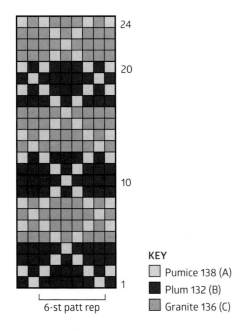

24
20
10
1

6-st patt rep

KEY
- ▫ Pumice 138 (A)
- ■ Plum 132 (B)
- ▪ Granite 136 (C)

POCKET LININGS (make 2)

With 4.5mm (US 7) needles and A, cast on 24 sts.

Beg with a k row work 31 rows in st st.

Inc row P3, [m1, p3] 7 times. *31 sts.*

Leave these sts on a holder.

LEFT FRONT

With 4mm (US 6) needles and D, cast on 67(73:79) sts.

Rib row 1 P1, [k1, p1] to end.

Rib row 2 K1, [p1, k1] to end.

These 2 rows form the rib.

Work a further 10 rows, inc one st at centre of last row. *68(74:80) sts.*

Change to 4.5mm (US 7) needles and work in patt from Chart.

Row 1 [Work across 6-st patt rep of row 1] 11(12:13) times, work 2 sts after patt rep.

Row 2 Work 2 sts before patt rep, [work across 6-st patt rep of row 2] 11(12:13) times.

These 2 rows **set** the chart for the 24-row patt.

Work a further 30 rows.

PLACE POCKET LINING

Next row Patt 20(23:26), place next 31 sts on a holder, patt 31 sts from pocket lining, then patt rem 17(20:23) sts.

Cont in patt until 28 rows fewer have been worked than on back to beg of armhole shaping, ending with a wrong side row.

SHAPE FRONT NECK

Next row Patt to last 2 sts, work 2 tog.

Work 1 row.

Rep the last 2 rows 13 times more.

54(60:66) sts.

SHAPE ARMHOLE AND FRONT NECK

Next row Cast off 9 (10:11) sts, patt to last 2 sts, work 2 tog. *44(49:54) sts.*

Next row Patt to end.

Dec one st at neck edge on 3rd and every foll 4th row;

at the same time dec one st at arm hole edge on next 6(8:10) rows, then 6 foll right side rows. *29 (30:33) sts.*

Keeping armhole edge straight cont to dec at neck edge on

every 2nd (4th;2nd) and foll 4th(0:4th) row until 27(29:31) sts rem.

Work straight until left front measures the same as back to shoulder shaping, ending at armhole edge.

SHAPE SHOULDER

Next row Cast off 9 sts, patt to end.

Work 1 row.

Next row Cast off 9(10:11) sts, patt to end.

Work 1 row.

Cast off rem 9(10:11) sts.

RIGHT FRONT

With 4mm (US 6) needles and D, cast on 67(73:79) sts.

Rib row 1 P1, [k1, p1] to end.

Rib row 2 K1, [p1, k1] to end.

These 2 rows form the rib.

Work a further 10 rows, inc one st at centre of last row. *68(74:80) sts.*

Change to 4.5mm (US 7) needles and work in patt from Chart.

Row 1 Work one st before patt rep, [work across 6-st patt rep of row 1] 11(12:13) times, work one st after patt rep.

Row 2 Work one st before patt rep, [work across 6-st patt rep of row 2] 11(12:13) times, work one st after patt rep.

These 2 rows **set** the chart for the 24-row patt.

Work a further 30 rows.

PLACE POCKET LINING

Next row Patt 17(20:23), place next 31 sts on a holder, patt 31 sts from pocket lining, then patt rem 20(23:26) sts.

Cont in patt until 28 rows fewer have been worked than on back to beg of armhole shaping, ending with a wrong side row.

SHAPE FRONT NECK

Next row Work 2 tog, patt to end.

Work 1 row.

Rep the last 2 rows 13 times.

Next row Work 2 tog, patt to end. 53 (59:65) sts.

SHAPE ARMHOLE AND FRONT NECK

Next row Cast off 9(10:11) sts, patt to end. *44(49:54) sts.*

Dec one st at neck edge on 3rd and every foll 4th row; **at the same time** dec one st at armhole edge on next 6(8:10) rows, then 6 foll right side rows.

Keeping armhole edge straight cont to dec at neck edge on 2nd(4th:2nd) and foll 4th(0:4th) row until 27(29:31) sts rem.

Work straight until right front measures the same as back to shoulder shaping, ending at armhole edge.

SHAPE SHOULDER

Next row Cast off 9 sts, patt to end.

Work 1 row.

Next row Cast off 9(10:11) sts, patt to end.

Work 1 row.

Cast off rem 9(10:11) sts.

BACK NECKBAND

With 4mm (US 6) needles and D, pick up and k43(45:47) sts evenly around back neck.

Rib row 1 K1, [p1, k1] to end.

Rib row 2 P1, [k1, p1] to end.

Rep the last 2 rows twice more and row 1 again.

Cast off in rib.

BUTTONBAND

With 4mm (US 6) needles and D, pick up and k56(58:60) sts up right front to beg of neck shaping, then 78(80:82) sts to shoulder. *134(138:142) sts.*

Rib row 1 [P1, k1] to end.

Rib row 2 K2, [p1, k1] to end.

Rep the last 2 rows twice more and row 1 again.

Cast off in rib.

BUTTONHOLE BAND

With 4mm (US 6) needles and D, pick up and k78(80:82) sts to beg of neck shaping, then 56(58:60) sts to cast on edge. *134(138:142) sts.*

Rib row 1 [K1, p1] to end.

Rib row 2 [K1, p1] to last 2 sts, k2.

Rib row 3 [K1, p1] to end.

Buttonhole row Rib to last 54(55:56) sts, [yf, rib 2tog, rib 8] 5 times, yf, rib 2tog, rib 2(3:4).

Work 3 rows in rib.

Cast off in rib.

ARMBANDS (both alike)

Join shoulder and neckband seams. With right side facing, using 4mm (US 6) needles and D, pick up and k128(136:144) sts evenly round armhole edge.

Rib row [K1, p1] to end.

Rep the last row 6 times more.

Cast off in rib.

POCKET TOPS (both alike)

With 4mm (US 6) needles and D, k31 sts from pocket front.

Rib row 1 K1, [p1, k1] to end.

Rib row 2 K2, p1, [k1, p1] to last 2 sts, k2.

Rib row 3 K1, [p1, k1] to end.

Cast off in rib.

TO MAKE UP

Join side and armband seams. Sew down pocket linings and pocket tops. Sew on buttons.

olav mug hug

MEASUREMENTS
To fit average size mug

YARN
1 x 50g balls of Rowan *Pure Wool Superwash DK* Flint 105
OR
1 x 50g balls of Rowan *Pure Wool Superwash DK* Grit 109
OR
1 x 50g balls of Rowan *Pure Wool Superwash DK* Gravel 108.

NEEDLES
Pair of 3.25mm (US 3) needles.

TENSION
24 sts and 40 rows to 10cm/4in square over patt using 3.25mm (US 3) needles, or size to obtain correct tension.

ABBREVIATIONS
Cr9FB Slip next 6 sts onto a cable needle and leave at front of work, k3, then slip the last 3 sts on the left of the cable needle back onto the left-hand needle, then leave the cable needle holding 3 sts at the back of work. Knit the 3 sts from left-hand needle, then knit the remaining 3 sts from cable needle.

Cr9BF Slip next 6 sts onto a cable needle and leave at back of work, k3, then slip the last 3 sts on the left of the cable needle back onto the left-hand needle, then leave the cable needle holding 3 sts at the front of work. Knit the 3 sts from left-hand needle, then knit the remaining 3 sts from cable needle.

See also page 93.

TO MAKE
With 3.25mm (US 3) needles cast on 19 sts.
Row 1 (rs) K1, * p1, k1; rep from * to end.
Row 2 P1, * k1, p1; rep from * to end.
These 2 rows form the rib.
Row 3 As row 1.
Row 4 Rib 8, m1, [rib 1, m1] 3 times, rib 8. *23 sts.*
Work in patt as folls:-
Row 1 (rs) Sl 1, k to end.
Row 2 Sl 1, k6, p9, k7.
Row 3 As row 1.
Row 4 As row 2.
Row 5 Sl 1, k6, Cr9FB, k7.
Row 6 As row 2.
Rows 7 to 12 As rows 1 and 2, three times.
Row 13 Sl 1, k6, Cr9BF, k7.
Row 14 As row 2.
Rows 15 and 16 As rows 1 and 2.
These 16 rows **set** the patt.
Repeat rows 1 to 16 five times more then rows 1 to 5 once more ending with a right side row.
Row 102 (ws) Sl 1, k6, p1, [p2tog] 4 times, p7. *19 sts.*
Beg with row 1 work 3 rows in rib.
Cast off ribwise.

TO MAKE UP
Join row ends of both rib sections.

jorgen slipover

SIZES

TO FIT BUST/CHEST

81	86	91	97	102	107	112	117	122	cm
32	34	36	38	40	42	44	46	48	in

ACTUAL MEASUREMENTS

Bust/Chest

91	95	99	103	107	112	116	120	124	cm
36	37½	39	40½	42	44	45¾	47¼	48¾	in

Length to back neck

51	53	55	57	59	61	63	65	67	cm
20	21	21½	22½	23¼	24	24¾	25½	26½	in

YARN

Rowan *Hemp Tweed*

His version

6(6:7:7:8:8:9:9:10) x 50g balls of Pumice 138 (A).

2(2:2:2:2:3:3:3:3) x 50g balls Treacle 134 (B).

Her version

6(6:7:7:8:8:9:9:10) x 50g balls Duck Egg 139 (A).

2(2:2:2:2:3:3:3:3) x 50g balls Teal 131 (B).

NEEDLES

Pair each of 3.75mm (US 5) and 4.5mm (US 7) knitting needles.

Cable needle

TENSION

19 sts and 25 rows to 10cm/4in square over st st using 4.5mm (US 7) needles, or size to obtain correct tension.

ABBREVIATIONS

C6F Slip next 3 sts onto a cable needle and leave at front of work, k3 then k3 from cable needle;

C6B Slip next 3 stitches onto a cable needle and leave at back of work, k3, then p3 from cable needle;

See also page 93.

CABLE PANEL (worked over 9 sts)

Row 1 K9.

Row 2 P9.

Row 3 C6B, k3.

Row 4 P9.

Row 5 K9.

Row 6 P9.

Row 7 K3, C6F.

Row 8 P9.

These 8 rows form the patt, and are repeated.

BACK

Using 3.75mm (US 5) needles and B cast on 111(115:119:123:127:131:135:139:143) sts.

Rib row 1 K1tbl, [p1, k1tbl] to end.

Rib row 2 P1, [k1, p1] to end.

Rep the last 2 rows 9 times more.

Break off B.

Join in A.

Change to 4.5mm (US 7) needles.

Work in patt.

Foundation row 1 (rs) K2, [k1tbl, k1] 4(5:6:7:8:9:10:11:12) times, k1, [work across row 1 of cable panel, k2, k1tbl, k1, k1tbl, k2] 5 times, work across row 1 of cable panel, k2, [k1tbl, k1] 4(5:6:7:8:9:10:11:12) times, k1.

Foundation row 2 K1, [p1, p1tbl] 4(5:6:7:8:9:10:11:12) times, p1, k1, [work across row 2 of cable panel, k1, p1, p1tbl, p1, p1tbl, p1, k1] 5 times, work across row 2 of cable panel, k1, [p1, p1tbl] 4(5:6:7:8:9:10:11:12) times, p1, k1.

Row 1 (rs) P2, [k1tbl, p1] 4(5:6:7:8:9:10:11:12) times, p1, [work across row 3 of cable panel, p2, k1tbl, p1, k1tbl, p2] 5 times, work across row 3 of cable panel, p2, [k1tbl, p1] 4(5:6:7:8:9:10:11:12) times, p1.

Row 2 K1, [p1, p1tbl] 4(5:6:7:8:9:10:11:12) times, p1, k1, [work across row 4 of cable panel, k1, p1, p1tbl1, p1, p1tbl, p1, k1] 5 times, work across row 4 of cable panel, k1, [p1, p1tbl] 4(5:6:7:8:9:10:11:12) times, p1, k1.

These 2 rows **place** the cable panel and form the patt between cable panels.

Cont in patt until work measures 32(33:34:35:36:37:38:39: 40)cm/12 ½(13:13½:13¾:14:14½:15:15¼:15¾)in from cast-on edge, ending with a wrong side row.

SHAPE ARMHOLES

Cast off 4(5:6:6:7:8:8:9:10) sts at beg of next 2 rows.
103(105:107:111:113:115:119:121:123) sts.

Next row K1, skpo, patt to last 3 sts, k2tog, k1.

Next row Patt to end.

Rep the last 2 rows 4(4:4:5:5:5:6:6:6) times more.
*93(95:97:99:101:103:105:107:109) sts **.*

Cont straight until back measures 51(53:55:57:59:61:63:65:67)cm/20(21:21½:22½:23¼:24:24¾: 25½:26½)in from cast-on edge, ending with a wrong side row.

SHAPE SHOULDERS AND BACK NECK

Next row Patt 32(33:33:34:34:35:35:36:36), turn and work on these sts for first side of back neck.

Dec one st at neck edge on next 3 rows.
29(30:30:31:31:32:32:33:33) sts.

SHAPE SHOULDER

Cast off 10 sts at beg of next and foll right side row.

Work 1 row.

Cast off rem 9(10:10:11:11:12:12:13:13) sts.

With right side facing, slip centre 29(29:31:31:33:33:35:35:37) sts onto a holder, rejoin yarn to rem sts, patt to end.

Dec one st at neck edge on next 3 rows.
29(30:30:31:31:32:32:33:33) sts.

Work 1 row.

SHAPE SHOULDER

Cast off 10 sts at beg of next and foll wrong side row.

Work 1 row.

Cast off rem 9(10:10:11:11:12:12:13:13) sts.

FRONT

Work as given for Back to **.

SHAPE FRONT NECK

Next row Patt 46(47:48:49:50:51:52:53:54) sts, turn and work on these sts for first side of front neck.

Dec one st at neck edge on every right side row until 29(30:30:31:31:32:32:33:33) sts rem.

Work straight until front measures the same as back to shoulder, ending at armhole edge.

SHAPE SHOULDER

Cast off 10 sts at beg of next and foll right side row.

Work 1 row.

Cast off rem 9(10:10:11:11:12:12:13:13) sts.

With right side facing, place centre st onto a safety pin, rejoin yarn to rem sts, patt to end.

Dec one st at neck edge on every right side row until 29(30:30:31:31:32:32:33:33) sts rem.

Work straight until front measures the same as back to shoulder, ending at armhole edge.

SHAPE SHOULDER

Cast off 10 sts at beg of next and foll wrong side row.

Work 1 row.

Cast off rem 9(10:10:11:11:12:12:13:13) sts.

NECKBAND

Join right shoulder seam.

With right side facing, using 3.75mm (US 5) needles and B, pick up and k47(49:51:51:53:55:55:57:57) sts down left side of front neck, one st from safety pin, pick up and k46(48:50:50:52:54:54:56:56) sts up right side of front neck, 8 sts down right side of back neck, k29(29:31:31:33:33:35:35:37) sts from back neck holder, pick up and k9 sts up left side of back neck.

140(144:150:150:156:160:162:166:168) sts.

Rib row [P1, k1] to end.

This row **sets** the rib.

Working in twisted rib as given for welts, work as folls:

Next row Rib 46(48:50:50:52:54:54:56:56) s2kpo, rib to end.

Next row Rib to end.

Next row Rib 45(47:49:49:51:53:53:55:55), s2kpo, rib to end.

Next row Rib to end.

Next row Rib 44(46:48:48:50:52:52:54:54), s2kpo, rib to end. *134(138:144:144:150:154:156:160:162) sts.*

Next row Rib to end.

Cast off in rib, dec on this row as before.

ARMBANDS (both alike)

Join left shoulder and neckband seam.

With right side facing, using 3.75mm (US 5) needles and B, pick up and k100(104:108:112:116:120:124:128:132) sts evenly all round armhole edge.

Rib row [K1, p1] to end.

Working in twisted rib as given for welts work a further 6 rows.

Cast off in rib.

TO MAKE UP

Join side and armband seams.

valentin hat

MEASUREMENTS

Two sizes to fit a woman's average-size head and a man's average-size head.

YARN

Rowan *Hemp Tweed*
2 x 50g balls of Duck Egg 139
OR
2 x 50g balls of Denim 133.

NEEDLES

Pair each 4mm (US 6) and 4.5mm (US 7) needles.
Cable needle.

TENSION

19 sts and 25 rows to 10cm/4in square over st st using
4.5mm (US 7) needles, or size to obtain correct tension.
22 sts and 26 rows to 10cm/4in square over patt using
4.5mm (US 7) needles, or size to obtain correct tension.

ABBREVIATIONS

C4B Cable 4 back, slip next 2 sts onto a cable needle and
hold at back of work, k2, then k2 from cable needle.
See page 93.

TO MAKE

With 4.5mm (US 7) needles cast on 106(114) sts.

Rib row 1 K2, [p2, k2] to end.

Rib row 2 P2, [k2, p2] to end.

These 2 rows form the rib.

Work a further 10 rows.

Change to 4mm (US 6) needles.

Work a further 12 rows, inc 5(6) sts evenly across last row.
111(120) sts.

Change to 4.5mm (US 7) needles.

Work in patt as follows:

Row 1 P1, [k3, p1, k4, p1] to last 2 sts, p2.

Row 2 K3, [p4, k5] to end.

Rows 3 and 4 As rows 1 and 2.

Row 5 P1, [k3, p1, C4B, p1] to last 2 sts, p2.

Row 6 As row 2.

Rows 7 and 8 As rows 1 and 2.

These 8 rows **set** the patt.

Work a further 20(28) rows in patt.

Dec row 1 P1, [k1, k2tog, p1, C4B, p1] to last 2 sts, p2.
99(107) sts.

Work 3 rows as set.

Dec row 2 P1, [k2tog, p1, k4, p1] to last 2 sts, p2. *87(94) sts.*

Work 3 rows as set.

SHAPE CROWN

Dec row 3 P1, * k1, p1, slip next 2 sts onto a cable needle
and hold at back of work, [k next st on left hand needle tog
with next st on cable needle] twice, p1; rep from * to last 2
sts, p2. *63(68) sts.*

Work 3 rows as set.

Dec row 4 P1, [p2tog, k2, p1] to last 2 sts, p2. *51(55) sts.*

Work 1 row as set.

Dec row 5 P1, [p1, k2tog, p1] to last 2 sts, p2. *39(42) sts.*

Work 1 row as set.

Dec row 6 P1, [p1, p2tog] to last 2 sts, p2. *27(29) sts.*

Dec row 7 K2, [k2tog] to last st, k1. *15(16) sts.*

Break off yarn, thread through rem sts. draw up and secure.

TO MAKE UP

Join seam, reversing seam for turn back.

Make a pompon, attach to crown of hat.

klaus scarf

MEASUREMENTS

Approx. 12.5cm/5in wide x 195cm/76¾in long.

YARN

3 x 100g balls of Rowan *Pure Wool Superwash Worsted*
Oats 152
OR
3 x 100g balls of Rowan *Pure Wool Superwash Worsted*
Mole 157.

NEEDLES

Pair of 4.5mm (US7) knitting needles.
Cable needle.

TENSION

20 sts and 25 rows to 10cm/4in over st st using 4.5mm
(US 7) needles, or size to obtain correct tension.

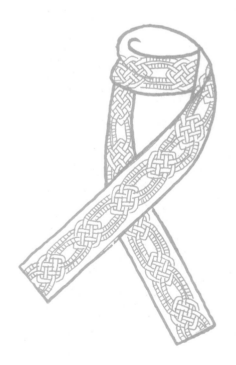

ABBREVIATIONS

Cr4R Slip next st onto a cable needle and leave at back of
work, k3, then p1 from cable needle.

Cr4L Slip next 3 sts onto a cable needle and leave at front
of work, p1, then k3 from cable needle.

T5R Slip next 2 sts onto a cable needle and leave at back
of work, k3, then p2 from cable needle.

T5L Slip next 3 sts onto a cable needle and leave at front of
work, p2, then k3 from cable needle.

C6B Slip next 3 sts onto a cable needle and leave at back
of work, k3 then k3 from cable needle.

C6F Slip next 3 sts onto a cable needle and leave at front
of work, k3 then k3 from cable needle.

Cr7F Slip next 4 sts onto a cable needle and leave at front
of work, k3 then slip last st on the left of the cable needle
back onto left hand needle and p this st from left hand
needle, then k3 from cable needle.

dec.7 Slip next 4 sts with yarn in front [RS] of work * pass
the 2nd stitch on right-hand needle over the 1st (centre)
stitch, slip the centre stitch back on to left-hand needle and
pass the 2nd stitch on left-hand needle over it * slip the
centre stitch back onto right-hand needle again and repeat
from * to * twice more. Pick up yarn and knit the centre
stitch.

c.d.i [k1tbl, k1] into next stitch, then insert left-hand needle
point behind the vertical strand that runs downward from
between the 2 sts just made, and k1tbl into this strand to
make the 3rd st of the group.

purl inc. [p1, yrn, p1] in next stitch.

wrap 3 Yrn, p3, then lift the yrn over these 3 sts and off
the needle.

See also page 93.

NOTE

When working from Chart odd numbered rows are read from right to left. Even numbered rows are read from left to right.

TO MAKE

With 4.5mm (US 7) needles cast on 39 sts.

Work in patt from Chart.

Row 1 (rs) Work across 39 sts of row 1.

Row 2 Work across 39 sts of row 2.

These 2 rows **set** the chart.

Cont in patt to end of row 36.

Now repeat rows 5 to 36 from Chart, 14 more times, then rows 1 and 2, twice more. Cast off ribwise.

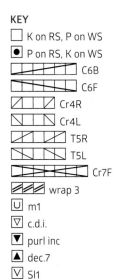

KEY

☐ K on RS, P on WS

⦿ P on RS, K on WS

C6B

C6F

Cr4R

Cr4L

T5R

T5L

Cr7F

wrap 3

Ⓤ m1

▽ c.d.i.

▼ purl inc

▲ dec.7

Ⓥ Sl1

⦁ K1tbl

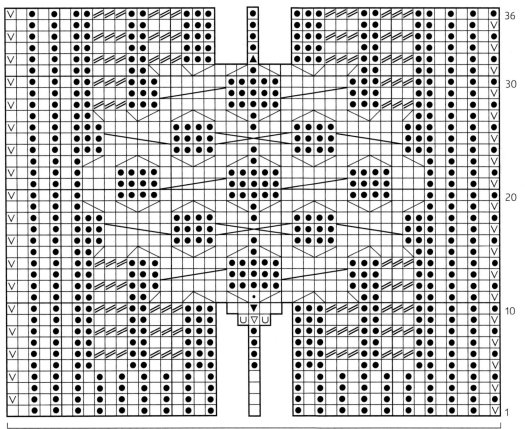

39-st patt rep

pine trees bottle tops

MEASUREMENTS

To fit average wine cork.

YARN

Oddments of Rowan *Felted Tweed* in two contrast colours (A and B) of your choice.

NEEDLES

Pair of 2.75mm (US 2) knitting needles.

EXTRAS

6 small beads.

TENSION

27 sts and 45 rows to 10cm/4in square over garter stitch using 2.75mm (US 2) needles, or size to obtain correct tension.

ABBREVIATIONS

See page 93.

NOTE

The knitting needs to be as tight as possible. If necessary, use a size smaller needle.

PINE TREE – LARGE STRIPE

With 2.75mm (US 2) needles and A, cast on 19 sts.

Row 1 (rs) Using A, knit.

Row 2 Using A, knit.

These 2 rows form the garter stitch patt.

Work a further 4 rows in A.

Join in B.

Work 6 rows in B.

Work 6 rows in A.

Rep last 12 rows once more.

Row 31 Using B, [k4, k2tog] 3 times, k1. *16 sts.*

Row 32 Using B, knit.

Work a further 4 rows in B.

Row 37 Using A, [k3, k2tog] 3 times, k1. *13 sts.*

Row 38 Using A, knit.

Work a further 4 rows in A.

Row 43 Using B, [k2, k2tog] 3 times, k1. *10 sts.*

Row 44 Using B, knit.

Work a further 4 rows in B.

Row 49 Using A, [k1, k2tog] 3 times, k1. *7 sts.*

Row 50 Using A, knit.

Work a further 4 rows in A.

Row 55 Using B, [k2tog] 3 times, k1. *4 sts.*

Row 56 Using B, knit.

Work a further 4 rows in B.

Row 61 Using B, k4tog and fasten off.

TO MAKE UP

Matching ridges of garter stitch and using a neat, mattress stitch, join row-ends of pine tree together.

Sew bead to top of tree.

PINE TREE – LARGE PLAIN

With 2.75mm (US 2) needles and A, cast on 19 sts.

Cont as for stripe version **BUT** using A only throughout.

PINE TREE – MEDIUM STRIPE

With 2.75mm needles and A, cast on 19 sts.

Row 1 (rs) Using A, knit.

Row 2 Using A, knit.

These 2 rows form the garter stitch.

Work a further 2 rows in A.

Join in B.

Work 4 rows in B.

Work 4 rows in A.

Rep last 8 rows once more.

Row 21 Using B, [k4, k2tog] 3 times, k1. *16 sts.*

Row 22 Using B, knit.

Work a further 2 rows in B.

Row 25 Using A, [k3, k2tog] 3 times, k1. *13 sts.*

Row 26 Using A, knit.

Work a further 2 rows in A.

Row 29 Using B, [k2, k2tog] 3 times, k1. *10 sts.*

Row 30 Using B, knit.

Work a further 2 rows in B.

Row 33 Using A, [k1, k2tog] 3 times, k1. *7 sts.*

Row 34 Using A, knit.

Work a further 2 rows in A.

Row 37 Using B, [k2tog] 3 times, k1. *4 sts.*

Row 38 Using B, knit.

Work a further 2 rows in B.

Row 41 Using B, k4tog and fasten off.

TO MAKE UP

Matching ridges of garter stitch and using a neat, mattress stitch, join row-ends of pine tree together.

Sew bead to top of tree.

PINE TREE – MEDIUM PLAIN

With 2.75mm (US 2) needles and A, cast on 19 sts.

Cont as for stripe version **BUT** using A only throughout.

PINE TREE – SMALL STRIPE

With 2.75mm (US 2) needles and A, cast on 19 sts.

Row 1 (rs) Using A, knit.

Row 2 Using A, knit.

These 2 rows form the garter stitch.

Work a further 2 rows in A.

Join in B.

Row 5 Using B, [k4, k2tog] 3 times, k1. *16 sts.*

Row 6 Using B, knit.

Work a further 2 rows in B.

Row 9 Using A, [k3, k2tog] 3 times, k1. *13 sts.*

Row 10 Using A, knit.

Work a further 2 rows in A.

Row 13 Using B, [k2, k2tog] 3 times, k1. *10 sts.*

Row 14 Using B, knit.

Work a further 2 rows in B.

Row 17 Using A, [k1, k2tog] 3 times, k1. *7 sts.*

Row 18 Using A, knit.

Work a further 2 rows in A.

Row 21 Using B, [k2tog] 3 times, k1. *4 sts.*

Row 22 Using B, knit.

Row 23 Using B, k4tog and fasten off.

TO MAKE UP

Matching ridges of garter stitch and using a neat, mattress stitch, join row-ends of pine tree together.

Sew bead to top of tree.

PINE TREE – SMALL PLAIN

With 2.75mm needles and A, cast on 19 sts.

Cont as for stripe version **BUT** using A only throughout.

ola scarf

MEASUREMENTS
Approx 15.5cm/6in wide, 164cm/64½in long.

YARN
3 x 100g balls of Rowan *Pure Wool Superwash Worsted* Almond 103.

NEEDLES
Pair of 4.5mm (US7) knitting needles.

EXTRAS
Beads

Debbie Abrahams – Size 6, Colour: 601 x 1 pack.

TENSION
20 sts and 25 rows to 10cm/4in square over st st using 4.5mm (US 7) needles, or size to obtain correct tension.

ABBREVIATIONS
Sl1 wyib Slip one stitch purlwise with yarn at back of work (WS of work).

Sl1 wyif Slip one stitch purlwise with yarn in front of work (**WS** of work).

Cr5 Drop first slip stitch off needle to front of work, slip next 3 sts, drop second slip stitch off needle to front of work, then holding the 3 knit sts on right-hand needle, pick up the first dropped st onto left hand needle, then slip the 3 sts back on to left-hand needle, then with point of right-hand needle, pick up the second dropped st and place it on left hand needle, then k5.

place bead On WS rows - place bead by taking yarn to RS of work, slipping bead up next to stitch just worked, slip next stitch purlways from left needle to right needle and bring yarn back to WS, leaving bead sitting in front of slipped stitch.

See also page 93.

Special Note for Beads

Before starting to knit, thread beads onto yarn. To do this, thread a fine sewing needle (one that will easily pass through the beads) with sewing thread. Knot ends of thread and then pass end of yarn through this loop. Thread a bead onto sewing thread and gently slide it along and onto knitting yarn. Continue in this way until required number of beads are on yarn.

NOTE
When working from Chart odd numbered rows are read from right to left. Even numbered rows are read from left to right.

TO MAKE

Thread on beads – see **Special Note for Beads**

With 4.5mm (US 7) needles cast on 49 sts.

Work in patt from Chart.

Row 1 (rs) Work 3 sts before patt rep, [work across row 1 of 6-st patt rep] 7 times, work 4 sts after patt rep.

Row 2 Work 4 sts before patt rep, [work across row 2 of 6-st patt rep] 7 times, work 4 sts after patt rep.

These 2 rows **set** the chart.

Cont in patt to end of row 14.

Now repeat rows 7 to 14 from Chart, 59 more times, then rows 7 to 10 from Chart once, ending with a wrong side row.

Now repeat rows 1 and 2 twice.

Cast-off in patt.

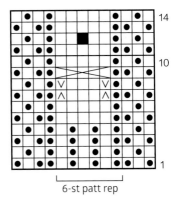

6-st patt rep

KEY

☐ K on RS, P on WS

⬤ P on RS, K on WS

△ Sl1 wyib

▽ Sl1 wyif

■ place bead

⬛⬛⬛ Cr5

useful information

SIZING

The instructions are given for the smallest size, and larger sizes follow in parentheses. If there is only one set of figures, it refers to all sizes. If a hyphen or a zero is given in an instruction for the size you are knitting, then that particular instruction does not apply to your size. Sizing information at the beginning of any garment pattern includes the actual bust measurement, the width of the garment at the bust, the length of the garment from shoulder to welt and the sleeve length, from the top of the armhole to the cuff.

TENSION

Tension controls both the shape and size of an article, so any variation, however slight, can distort the finished piece of knitting. For garments, this can be crucial so you need to ensure you can match the tension given at the start of each pattern. To check your tension, knit a square in the pattern stitch and/or stocking stitch of perhaps 5–10 more stitches and 5–10 more rows than those given in the tension note. Press the finished square under a damp cloth and mark out the central 10cm/4in square with pins. If you have more stitches to 10cm/4in than the given tension, try again using thicker needles. If you have fewer stitches than the given tension, try again using finer needles. Once you have achieved the correct tension, your garment will be knitted to the measurements given.

CABLE PATTERNS

Cable stitch patterns allow you to twist the stitches in various ways, to create decorative effects to give an interesting rope-like structure to the knitting. The cables can be thin and fine (just a couple of stitches wide) or big and chunky (up to 8 stitches or more). To work cables, you need to hold the appropriate number of stitches that form the cable twist (abbreviated in pattern as C)

on a separate small cable needle, while you knit behind or in front of them. You then knit the stitches off the cable needle before continuing to knit the remaining stitches in the row. Depending on whether the cable needle is at the front or the back of the work, the cables will twist to the left or right but the principle remains the same. A four-stitch cable will be abbreviated as C4F or C4B, depending on whether the cable needle is held to the front or back of the work. Abbreviations for the variations of cable, cross and twisted stitches are given in each pattern.

FAIRISLE

When you are working a pattern with two or more repeating colours in the same row, you need to strand the yarn not in use behind the stitches being worked. This needs to be done with care, loosely enough to ensure that the strands not in use do not tighten and pucker the front of the knitting. To do this you need to treat the yarns not in use, known a 'floating yarns', as if they were one yarn and spread the stitches as you work to their correct width to keep them elastic. If you tend to knit colourwork too tightly, increase your needle size for the colourwork section.

INTARSIA

This allows you to join in new yarns in the middle of rows where a new colour extends over more than 5 stitches or so. The simplest method is to cut short lengths of yarn for each block of colour and bind each them into small bobbins. Work across the row, joining in colours from bobbins as required, twisting them around each other on the WS of the work to avoid any gaps. After you have completed the piece of knitting, neaten up the loose ends by darning along the colour joins.When working in Intarsia, check that the tension is correct; it may vary from the plain stocking stitch if both are used in the pattern.

FINISHING METHODS

Pressing

Block out each piece of knitting by pinning it on a board to the correct measurements in the pattern. Then lightly press it according to the ball band instructions, omitting any ribbed areas. Take special care to press the edges, as this makes sewing up easier and neater. If you cannot press the fabric, then cover the knitted fabric with a damp cloth and allow it to stand for a couple of hours. Darn in all ends neatly along the selvedge edge or a colour join.

Stitching seams

When you stitch the pieces together, remember to match any areas of colour and texture carefully where they meet. Using a special seam stitch, called mattress stitch, creates the neatest flattest seam. After all the seams are complete, press the seams and hems. Lastly, sew on the buttons to correspond with the positions of the buttonholes.

ABBREVIATIONS

alt	alternate
approx	approximately
beg	begin(s)(ning)
cm	centimetres
cont	continu(e)(ing)
dec	decreas(e)(ing)
foll(s)	follow(s)(ing)
g	gram
g-st	garter stitch
in	inch(es)
inc	increas(e)(ing)
k	knit
k2tog	knit next 2 sts together
mm	millimetres
m1	make one st by picking up horizontal loop before next st and knitting into back of it
m1pw	make one st by picking up horizontal loop before next st and purling into back of it

0	no stitches
p	purl
patt	pattern
p2tog	purl next 2 sts together
psso	pass slipped stitch over
rem	remain(s)(ing)
rep	repeat
RS	right side
skpo	sl 1, k1, pass slipped stitch over
s2kpo	slip the next 2 sts as if to k them tog, k1 then pass slipped stitches over
Sl1	slip one st
st(s)	stitch(es)
St st	stocking stitch (1 row knit, 1 row purl)
tbl	through back of loop(s)
tog	together
WS	wrong side
yd	yard(s)
yf	yarn forward
yo	yarn oveyrn yarn round needle
ytf	with yarn to front
ytb	with yarn to back
[ ]/*	repeat instructions within square brackets or between asterisk

stockists

AUSTRALIA
Australian Country Spinners, Pty Ltd, Level 7, 409 St. Kilda Road,
Melbourne Vic 3004.
Tel: 03 9380 3888   Fax: 03 9820 0989
Email: customerservice@auspinners.com.au

AUSTRIA
MEZ Harlander GmbH, Schulhof 6, 1. Stock, 1010 Wien, Austria
Tel: +00800 26 27 28 00   Fax: (00) 49 7644 802-133
Email: verkauf.harlander@mezcrafts.com   Web: www.mezcrafts.at

BELGIUM
MEZ crafts Belgium NV, c/o MEZ GmbH, Kaiserstr.1, 79341
Kenzingen, Germany
Tel: 0032 (0) 800 77 89 2   Fax: 00 49 7644 802 133
Email: sales.be-nl@mezcrafts.com   Web: www.mezcrafts.be

BULGARIA
MEZ Crafts Bulgaria EOOD, Bul. Rozhen 25A, BG-1220 Sofia, Bulgaria
Tel: +359 2 439 24 24   Fax: +359 2 439 24 28
Email: office.bg@mezcrafts.com

CANADA
Westminster Fibers, 10 Roybridge Gate, Suite 200, Vaughan,
Ontario L4H 3M8
Tel: (800) 263-2354   Fax: 905-856-6184
Email: info@westminsterfibers.com

CHINA
Commercial agent Mr Victor Li, c/o MEZ GmbH Germany, Kaiserstr. 1,
79341 Kenzingen, Germany
Tel: (86- 21) 13816681825   Email: victor.li@mezcrafts.com

CHINA
SHANGHAI YUJUN CO.,LTD., Room 701 Wangjiao Plaza, No.175
Yan'an(E), 200002 Shanghai, China
Tel: +86 2163739785   Email: jessechang@vip.163.com

CYPRUS
MEZ Crafts Bulgaria EOOD, Bul. Rozhen 25A, BG-1220 Sofia, Bulgaria
Tel: +359 2 439 24 24   Fax: +359 2 439 24 28
Email: office.bg@mezcrafts.com

CZECH REPUBLIC
Coats Czecho s.r.o.Staré Mesto 246 569 32
Tel: (420) 461616633   Email: galanterie@coats.com

DENMARK
Carl J. Permin A/S Egegaardsvej 28 DK-2610 Rødovre
Tel: (45) 36 72 12 00   E-mail: permin@permin.dk

ESTONIA
MEZ Crafts Estonia OÜ, Ampri tee 9/4, 74001 Viimsi Harjumaa
Tel: +372 630 6252   Email: info.ee@mezcrafts.com
Web: www.coatscrafts.co.ee

FINLAND
MEZ Crafts Finland Oy, Huhtimontie 6, 04200 Kerava
Tel: (358) 9 274 871   Email: sales.fi@mezcrafts.com
Web: www.coatscrafts.fi

FRANCE
3bcom, 35 avenue de Larrieu, 31094 Toulouse cedex 01
Tel: 0033 (0) 562 202 096   Email: Commercial@3b-com.com

GERMANY
MEZ GmbH, Kaiserstr. 1, 79341 Kenzingen
Tel: 0049 7644 802 222   Email: kenzingen.vertrieb@mezcrafts.com
Fax: 0049 7644 802 300   Web: www.mezcrafts.de

GREECE
MEZ Crafts Bulgaria EOOD, Bul. Rozhen 25A, BG-1220 Sofia,
Bulgaria
Tel: +359 2 439 24 24   Fax: +359 2 439 24 28
Email: office.bg@mezcrafts.com

HOLLAND
G. Brouwer & Zn B.V., Oudhuijzerweg 69, 3648 AB Wilnis,
Netherlands
Tel: 0031 (0) 297-281 557   Email: info@gbrouwer.nl

HONG KONG
East Unity Company Ltd, Unit B2, 7/F., Block B, Kailey Industrial
Centre, 12 Fung Yip Street, Chai Wan
Tel: (852)2869 7110   Email: eastunityco@yahoo.com.hk

ICELAND
Carl J. Permin A/S Egegaardsvej 28 DK-2610 Rødovre
Tel: (45) 36 72 12 00   Email: permin@permin.dk

ITALY
Mez Cucirini Italy Srl, Viale Sarca, 223, 20126 MILANO
Tel: 02 636151   Fax: 02 66111701

JAPAN
Hobbyra Hobbyre Corporation, 23-37, 5-Chome, Higashi-Ohi,
Shinagawa-Ku, 1400011 Tokyo.
Tel: +81334721104
Daidoh International, 3-8-11 Kudanminami Chiyodaku, Hiei Kudan
Bldg 5F, 1018619 Tokyo.
Tel: +81-3-3222-7076   Fax: +81-3-3222-7066

KOREA
My Knit Studio, 3F, 144 Gwanhun-Dong, 110-300 Jongno-Gu, Seoul
Tel: 82-2-722-0006 Email: myknit@myknit.com
Web: www.myknit.com

LATVIA
Coats Latvija SIA, Mukusalas str. 41 b, Riga LV-1004
Tel: +371 67 625173 Fax: +371 67 892758
Email: info.latvia@coats.com Web: www.coatscrafts.lv

LEBANON
y.knot, Saifi Village, Mkhalissiya Street 162, Beirut
Tel: (961) 1 992211 Fax: (961) 1 315553 Email: y.knot@cyberia.net.lb

LITHUANIA and RUSSIA
MEZ Crafts Lithuania UAB, A. Juozapaviciaus str. 6/2, LT-09310
Vilnius
Tel: +370 527 30971 Fax: +370 527 2305
Email: info.lt@mezcrafts.com Web: www.coatscrafts.lt

LUXEMBOURG
Coats N.V., c/o Coats GmbH, Kaiserstr.1, 79341 Kenzingen, Germany
Tel: 00 49 7644 802 222 Fax: 00 49 7644 802 133
Email: sales.coatsninove@coats.com Web: www.coatscrafts.be

MEXICO
Estambres Crochet SA de CV, Aaron Saenz 1891-7Pte, 64650
MONTERREY
Tel: +52 (81) 8335-3870 Email: abremer@redmundial.com.mx

NEW ZEALAND
ACS New Zealand, P.O Box 76199, Northwood, Christchurch
Tel: 64 3 323 6665 Fax: 64 3 323 6660 Email: lynn@impactmg.co.nz

NORWAY
Carl J. Permin A/S Egegaardsvej 28 DK-2610 Rødovre
Tel: (45) 36 72 12 00 E-mail: permin@permin.dk

PORTUGAL
Mez Crafts Portugal, Lda – Av. Vasco da Gama, 774-4431-059 V.N,
Gaia
Tel: 00 351 223 770700 Email: sales.iberia@mezcrafts.com

SINGAPORE
Golden Dragon Store, BLK 203 Henderson Rd #07-02, 159546
Henderson Indurstrial Park
Tel: (65) 62753517 Fax: (65) 62767112 Email: gdscraft@hotmail.com

SLOVAKIA
MEZ Crafts Slovakia, s.r.o. Seberíniho 1, 821 03 Bratislava
Tel: +421 2 32 30 31 19 Email: galanteria@mezcrafts.com

SOUTH AFRICA
Arthur Bales LTD, 62 4th Avenue, Linden 2195
Tel: (27) 11 888 2401 Fax: (27) 11 782 6137 Email: arthurb@new.co.za
Web: www.arthurbales.co.za

SPAIN
MEZ Fabra Spain S.A, Avda Meridiana 350, pta 13 D, 08027
Barcelona
Tel: +34 932908400 Fax: +34 932908409
Email: atencion.clientes@mezcrafts.com

SWEDEN
Carl J. Permin A/S Egegaardsvej 28 DK-2610 Rødovre
Tel: (45) 36 72 12 00 Email: permin@permin.dk

SWITZERLAND
MEZ Crafts Switzerland GmbH, Stroppelstrasse20, 5417
Untersiggenthal
Tel: +41 00800 2627 2800 Fax: 0049 7644 802 133
Email: verkauf.ch@mezcrafts.com Web: www.mezcrafts.ch

TURKEY
MEZ Crafts Tekstil A.Ş, Kavacık Mahallesi, Ekinciler Cad. Necip Fazıl
Sok.
No.8 Kat: 5, 34810 Beykoz/İstanbul
Tel: +90 216 425 88 10 Web: www.mezcrafts.com

TAIWAN
Cactus Quality Co Ltd, 7FL-2, No. 140, Sec.2 Roosevelt Rd, Taipei,
10084 Taiwan, R.O.C.
Tel: 00886-2-23656527 Fax: 886-2-23656503
Email: cqcl@ms17.hinet.net

THAILAND
Global Wide Trading, 10 Lad Prao Soi 88, Bangkok 10310
Tel: 00 662 933 9019 Fax: 00 662 933 9110
Email: global.wide@yahoo.com

U.S.A.
Westminster Fibers, 8 Shelter Drive, Greer, South Carolina, 29650
Tel: (800) 445-9276 Fax: 864-879-9432
Email: info@westminsterfibers.com

U.K
Coats Crafts UK, Green Lane Mill, Holmfirth, West Yorkshire,
England HD9 2DX
Tel: +44 (0) 1484 681881 Fax: +44 (0) 1484 687920
Email: ccuk.sales@coats.com Web: www.knitrowan.com

For more stockists in all countries please visit www.rowan.com

YARNS

The following Rowan yarns have been used in this book:

Big Wool

100% Merino wool; 100g balls; 80m/87yd per ball;
7½-9sts and 10-12½rows to 10cm/4in using 10 or 15mm
(US 15-19) needles.

Creative Focus Worsted

75% wool; 25% alpaca; 100g balls; 200m/220yd per ball;
20sts and 24 rows to 10cm/4in using 4.5mm (US 7) needles.

Felted Tweed

Merino Wool 50%; Alpaca: 25%; Viscose: 25%;
50g balls; 175m/191yd per ball; 22-24sts and 30-32 rows to
10cm/4in using 3.75-4mm (US 5-6) needles.

Hemp Tweed

Wool: 75%; True Hemp: 25%; 50g balls; 95m/104yd per ball;
19sts and 25 rows to 10cm/4in using 4.5mm (US 7) needles.

Pure Cashmere DK

Cashmere: 100%; 25g balls; 112m/122yd per ball; 22 sts and
30 rows to 10cm/4in using 4mm (US 6) needles.

Pure Wool Superwash DK

100% Superwash Wool; 50g balls; 130m/142yd per ball;
22sts and 30 rows to 10cm/4in using 4mm (US size 6)
needles.

Pure Wool Superwash Worsted

Superwash Wool 100%; 100g balls; 200m/219yd per ball;
20sts and 25rows to 10cm/4in using 4.5mm (US 7) needles.

ACKNOWLEDGMENTS

A huge and heartfelt thank you to the following team of people: Steven and Susan for
their wonderful photography, art direction and styling; our lovely models Harriet and
Lee; Anne for working her magic on the fabulous layouts; Hazel for her Scandinavian
photography; Penny Hill and her team for the superb patterns and sample knitting;
Frances for the beautifully knitted swatches; Jill for her diligent editing and checking;
Sharon, David and the entire Rowan team for their continuous support and, finally,
Penny and Lee for allowing us to take pictures in their stylish Ilfracombe home.